baths
DESIGNS FOR LIVING

BATHS DESIGNS FOR LIVING®

Contributing Editor: Catherine M. Staub, Lexicon
Consulting, Inc.
Contributing Associate Editor: Julie Collins, Lexicon
Consulting, Inc.
Contributing Writer: Martin Miller
Contributing Assistants: Randall Noblet, Holly Reynolds,
Emma Sarran, Lexicon Consulting, Inc.
Contributing Graphic Designer: On-Purpos, Inc.
Copy Chief: Terri Fredrickson
Publishing Operations Manager: Karen Schirm
Senior Editor, Asset and Information Manager: Phillip Morgan
Edit and Design Coordinator: Mary Lee Gavin
Editorial and Design Assistant: Renee E. McAtee
Book Production Managers: Pam Kvitne, Marjorie J.
Schenkelberg, Rick von Holdt, Mark Weaver
Contributing Copy Editor: Nancy Evans
Contributing Proofreaders: Tom Blackett, Heidi Johnson,
Michele Pettinger
Contributing Indexer: Stephanie Reymann
Contributing Photographer: Tim Abramowitz,
Abramowitz Creative Studios
Set Production: Tim Arends
Stylist: Elizabeth Saunders
Additional Contributing Photography: Image Studios
Account Executive: Lisa Egan
Photography: Bill Rein
Assistant: Bill Kapinski
Set Design: Julie Gardner, Terri Neer
Set Construction: Rick Nadke
Stylists: Julie Gardner, Vicki Sumwalt

Meredith® Books

Executive Director, Editorial: Gregory H. Kayko
Executive Director, Design: Matt Strelecki
Managing Editor: Amy Tincher-Durik
Executive Editor/Group Manager: Benjamin W. Allen
Senior Associate Design Director: Doug Samuelson
Marketing Product Manager: Brent Wiersma
National Marketing Manager-Home Depot: Suzy Johnson

Publisher and Editor in Chief: James D. Blume
Editorial Director: Linda Raglan Cunningham
Executive Director, Marketing: Steve Malone
Executive Director, New Business Development: Todd M. Davis
Director, Sales-Home Depot: Robb Morris
Executive Director, Sales: Ken Zagor
Director, Operations: George A. Susral
Director, Production: Douglas M. Johnston
Director, Marketing: Amy Nichols
Business Director: Jim Leonard
Vice President and General Manager: Douglas J. Guendel

Meredith Publishing Group

President: Jack Griffin
Senior Vice President: Bob Mate

Meredith Corporation

Chairman and Chief Executive Officer: William T. Kerr
President and Chief Operating Officer: Stephen M. Lacy
In Memoriam: E.T. Meredith III (1933–2003)

The Home Depot®

Marketing Manager: Tom Sattler
© Copyright 2006 by Homer TLC, Inc.
First Edition.
All rights reserved.
Printed in the United States of America.
Library of Congress Control Number: 2006921274
ISBN-13: 978-0-696-22880-3
ISBN-10: 0-696-22880-7
The Home Depot® is a registered trademark of
Homer TLC, Inc.

Distributed by Meredith Corporation.
Meredith Corporation is not affiliated with The Home Depot®.

We are dedicated to providing inspiring, accurate and
helpful do-it-yourself information. We welcome your
comments about improving this book and ideas for other
books we might offer to home improvement enthusiasts.
Contact us by any of these methods:
Leave a voice message at: 800/678-2093
Write to:
Meredith Books, Home Depot Books
1716 Locust St.
Des Moines, IA 50309–3023
Send e-mail to: hi123@mdp.com.

contents

how to use this book

Improving your bathroom is an investment in the equity of your home and your quality of life, as well as a reflection of your style and taste. Remodeling and updating an existing bathroom or building a new one can be one of the largest single investments that you will make. The first step in making your dream bathroom a reality is finding a source of inspiration.

That's why the designers and associates at The Home Depot® have put together a collection of attractive and functional bathroom designs in one easy-to-use book. *Baths Designs for Living* will inspire you with hundreds of photos and ideas to create an ideal bathroom for your home and your lifestyle.

So whether you intend to design all or part of the bathroom yourself or plan to use the services of an architect or designer, you'll need a resource for ideas and some good advice on the latest possibilities for bathroom designs and styles.

STYLE-FUNCTION-DETAILS.

A bathroom design that works as well as you want it to is more than a floor plan and materials order; it's a comprehensive design that will turn your dream into reality. A good bathroom concept is a combination of style, function, and details. It's the result of defining your personal style and taste, considering how you and your family want to use the space now and in the future, and remembering the fine elements that will make the space complete.

Style. The style of your bathroom is a top priority. A decorating scheme can begin with a specific color, texture, or theme you want in your bathroom. With the style in place, decisions about sinks and faucets, fixtures, finishes, cabinetry, and floors will be easier. How much time and effort is put into this phase will ultimately define how happy you'll be in your new bathroom.

Function. Style is important, but make sure the components of your bathroom are functional as well. Consider various elements and how they can aid the function and accessibility of your bathroom. Remember to design for each member of your family who will use the room, taking individual needs into consideration.

Details. To get exactly what you want, you have to consider every element that will be part of your new bathroom, including cabinets, countertops, plumbing and fixtures, floors, color, texture, lighting, surfaces, and window treatments. The purposeful combination of these elements creates your style and unifies your bathroom.

ideas

All successful bathroom designs start with the answer to one question: "What do you want from this room?" Your response affects everything from the colors on the walls to the shape of the faucets. Explore the baths on the following pages—which blend style and function—to find inspiration for your bathroom design.

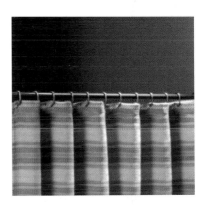

SPECIALTY FIXTURES
(RIGHT) This ceiling-mount bath filler simplifies this space by removing the typical faucet while providing a striking design element to the bath.

focal point

WATER DISPLAY. If your idea of a soothing end to the day is a retreat to the bathtub, make it the focal point of the room. In this bathroom a freestanding tub that fills from a ceiling-mount spout takes center stage. The filler—which requires a ceiling height less than 9 feet—puts the usual faucet out of sight. The edge-free glass shower wall is barely visible, giving the person showering an unobstructed view of the entire bath.

TEXTURAL INTEREST. Earthy slate walls, dark woods, and brushed-chrome accessories lend visual interest to this room. Slate naturally resists water and bacteria and brings the outdoors into this peaceful bath.

CREATE CONTRAST (LEFT)
Dark wood partnered with white cast iron is an eyecatching combination for the bathtub.

PRIVACY, PLEASE (BELOW)

A sliding door tucks away the toilet and bidet in this bathroom and reveals a linen closet. This solution is more sophisticated than a regular door but still provides privacy.

NECESSITY FIRST

(RIGHT) Cumbersome shower doors or bulky shower curtains don't inhibit the style or function of this room. Two glass walls are a better fit for the shower in this serene bath.

MAKE IT NATURAL (LEFT)

Derived from sediments of clay and fine silt, slate is the perfect wallcovering for a bathroom. It is stain-resistant, easily maintained, and available in multiple colors.

worn & modern

MIXING STYLES. Rustic and modern don't usually go hand in hand, but this bathroom successfully defines the unconventional combination. The clean lines of the steam shower and the polished chrome faucets contribute urban overtones, while deep red walls, rough-sawn cedar beams, and aged wooden pieces add rugged style.

CREATING CHARACTER. Achieve a worn look to your fixtures without going antiquing. In this bath, for example, the vanity was made from new wood that was distressed to look old. Be careful not to go overboard with the aging. The look complements the rustic red walls and evokes a homey feel. Clean lines and simple pieces provide contrast to rugged aspects and keep the space from looking chaotic.

EFFECTIVE MIX (LEFT) Aged elements combine with modern fixtures to deliver a unique feel in this bathroom. Custom-aged wood and simple sinks and faucets incorporate both rustic and contemporary style.

COZY SPACE (ABOVE) Simple additions to a space can significantly change the feel. This bath has high ceilings, but wooden beams just above door level create intimacy in the spacious area. A pocket door provides privacy in the toilet area and allows more efficient use of the space.

LESS IS MORE (ABOVE) This tub is inviting because of its minimalist surround and faucets that suggest a relaxing retreat. More detail would have looked too fussy in this design.

LIGHTEN UP Smooth white basins paired with distressed, dark-stained wood contribute visual drama to the vanity.

SUIT YOUR STYLE (BELOW) The master bath is a personal retreat and an ideal place to make a design statement. Unique elements such as the glass-block vanity and grass-motif fabric shade on the linen closet door provide distinct personality in this bathroom.

DURABLE DESIGN (LEFT) Although the vanity is the focal point, other thoughtful choices add to the function of this bath. Aluminum blinds fit the modern style of the room and match the aluminum edges of the lavatory base. The durable, antistatic finish repels dust and is scratch- and stain-resistant.

SHOWER WITH ELEGANCE
(ABOVE) This partial glass-block shower wall features a simple tempered glass shelf for toiletries as well as modest white matte floor tiles.

artful approach

FUNCTIONAL DESIGN. Artistry is not limited to the living room. The bathroom can be a perfect outlet for functional art. For example, this bath includes contemporary fixtures and design that contribute to a distinct look. The countertop lavatory exudes sophistication. While functional, the simple basin also possesses lines resembling an abstract sculpture. Glass block adds another modern aspect to the room and allows light to filter through the space. The glass-block vanity and shower wall add texture and style.

NATURAL COVER-UP. Look for chances to create art throughout your bath. A decorative fabric panel separates this bath's linen closet from the rest of the space. If your bathroom design is simple, something unusual such as this panel can add a tasteful accent. The fabric's light blue background also provides continuity between the main bath area and the light blue shower walls.

STAINED WOOD (BELOW) Custom cabinets with contrasting stains and woods create an elegant yet playful look for this bathroom. Changing shape, size, and fronts of the cabinets furthers the eclectic look.

SUBTLE BACKDROP (RIGHT) Neutral, warm-toned ceramic tile subtly complements the warm hues of the cabinetry and walls. A recessed toilet niche provides a touch of privacy.

creative storage

GEOMETRIC DESIGN. If you have no room for a linen closet to hide bath necessities, take note of the ample and stylish storage options in this bathroom. Traditional cider-stained maple and cinnamon-stained cherry cabinets pair in a mixture of shapes and sizes for a pleasing geometric look in the vanity area. Floor-to-ceiling custom cabinets separate the two vanities and provide space to store typical bathroom clutter. The combination of glass-, open-, and wood-front cabinets creates an eclectic look that adds playfulness to the setting. Above the two vanities, horizontal windows with frosted, grooved glass minimize visibility while allowing light into the room.

SPACE FOR RELAXATION. Even in this modest-size bath, a whirlpool tub set into a niche creates a relaxation sanctuary with its six jets and 18 different settings. Its classic architectural styling matches the other fixtures in the room.

TASTEFUL STORAGE (ABOVE AND OPPOSITE)
This built-in unit tucked into a recess across
from the tub looks like a freestanding piece
thanks to two types of wood with two stains.
Shelves display accessories and baskets behind
stained-glass inserts add texture.

QUALITY QUARTZ
(ABOVE) These quartz
countertops will stand
up to wear and tear
in the bathroom. The
rich color combination
coordinates with the
walls and cabinets, and
the pattern disguises
any nicks and scrapes.

EASY DOES IT (LEFT)
Pullout baskets make
stowing laundry a snap
and keep it hidden until
wash day. Simple drawers
utilize storage space to
its fullest capacity.

golden glow

COLOR CUES. Every moment in this bathroom is bound to be cheerful thanks to its sunny yellow and white color scheme. Tall white wainscoting topped with a panel ledge pairs with bright yellow walls to create a classic backdrop. Painting only the tops of the walls ensures the color doesn't overwhelm the space. The flooring, a wood-tone vinyl, balances the bright yellow without appearing too dark. Even the bathroom fixtures match—the toilet, tub, and sinks are all a sunny, subdued version of the wall color.

MADE FOR TWO. Back-to-back vanities provide separate grooming areas for this master bath's occupants. The vanities share a common wall and plumbing, and each spot includes its own window, pedestal sink, mirror, and towel bar. Although some back-to-back vanities are open to allow occupants to converse while grooming, this solid wall offers complete privacy. A metal stand at the end of the wall holds towels shared by both occupants. While not completely separated from the rest of the bath, the toilet is set back to create a semblance of privacy in the relatively open space.

GOLD AND GREEN (LEFT) Light streams into this sunny bathroom through windows beside each vanity area. Green towels, rugs, and robes are a natural accent to the bathroom's yellow tones.

PICTURE PERFECT

(LEFT) Individual shapes create a separate composition within the overall design. This pedestal sink visually supports the glass shelf, black tile border, oval mirror, and twin sconces.

retro decorate

EDGES OF INSPIRATION. Take cues for your new bathroom from the overall style of your house. The retro Art Deco design of this bath perfectly complements the 1930s home where it's located.

Because this is a small guest bath, the design elements must enhance yet not overwhelm the space. Art Deco makes this easy—it's a spare style with machine-made edges, angles, and surfaces, simple geometries, and uncomplicated contrasts that create a space with a unique identity.

INCHES MATTER. In a small bath inches are blessings. You'll be grateful to find a half inch here, a quarter inch there. Those small dimensions make a huge difference in whether the bathroom fixtures fit and if they look cramped or just right. Slim-line sinks and toilets help too. And because guest baths need little storage, doing without a closet or shelving can free up the space you need to make the room look comfortable.

PLANNING CONVENIENCE (BELOW) One-handled faucets are easier to use than two-handled units, and polished chrome cleans up easily.

FLUTED FINESSE (BELOW) A fluted showerhead nicely complements the bath's other fixtures.

JUST FOR FUN Uncomplicated design styles offer lots of latitude for subtle humor. Whatever this penguin is doing here—whether standing guard or simply waiting for a swim—it's sure to conjure a smile from guests.

SIMPLE CONTRASTS

When set against the white background, black tiles that define the walls and floor create visual contrasts. Details such as the black and white towels impact the design unlike any other colors would.

HANDLED WITH CARE (ABOVE AND RIGHT) Sink fixtures contribute to the overall style of a bathroom. Even the toilet paper holder is both functional and stylish because it matches the other accessories.

USEFUL ACCENTS (LEFT) This period-style clock helps keep the morning routine on schedule. Its rounded form lends subtle contrast to the harder edges of the bath's Art Deco style.

POINTS OF VIEW

(RIGHT) Mirrors swing out at virtually any angle above each sink, providing various points of view and degrees of magnification.

MORE THAN A LEDGE (LEFT) A wide ledge around the tub is used for built-in seating and as an easy-to-reach spot for towels.

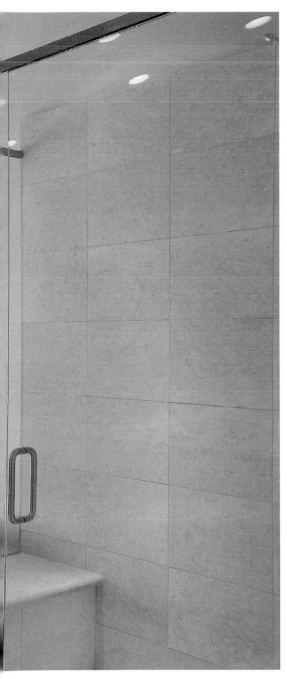

FOR SHOWERS TOO (LEFT) When there's no time for soaking, the nearby shower is available. A glass enclosure separates the shower without obstructing views.

all to yourself

PRIVATE ENCLAVE. A whirlpool tub located in the corner of this master bath makes the space feel like a private getaway. Pair soothing colors with customized luxuries for relaxation anytime. Enhancing the spa feeling, natural light filters through a glass-block window—lending privacy without blocking light. Subdued lights and speakers set into the ceiling further enhance the mood. Although the soffit ceiling was built primarily to accommodate wiring, its contours add a modern line overhead.

OPENLY PRIVATE. The same light that fills the tub corner also illuminates the adjacent glass-walled shower. To create continuity between the two bathing areas, travertine tiles adorn both the tub and shower surrounds, and the wide ledge around the tub continues into the shower to form a bench.

Unlike the open nature of the bathing areas, the toilet is located in a separate room between the vanity and the tub, providing the necessary measure of privacy.

water feature

GO WITH THE FLOW. Fixtures that provide soothing relief take center stage in this master bathroom retreat. The whirlpool tub allows for relaxing soaks and a wide tub deck provides room for tubside candles and bath products. In a separate shower compartment, multiple showerheads including three water tile sprayfaces relax tired muscles. Separate shower and tub spaces and two sinks situated in a generous vanity make this a comfortable spot for two people to prepare for the day.

SPRAY TILES (RIGHT) This shower features three complementary sources of water—a wall-mount showerhead, a hand-held sprayer, and spray tiles mounted into the wall of the shower. The tiles each have 54 spray nozzles.

CALMING SOAK (BELOW) This large whirlpool tub is an ideal respite for the end of a busy day. The location of the faucet at the corner of the tub makes it simple to draw a bath from outside of the fixture. This placement also frees access space along the side of the tub.

STRIKING CONTRAST This dark wood vanity becomes the focal point in an otherwise neutral-color bathroom. Highlighting the stain of the wood with the mirror frames helps unify the design. Ample storage beneath the sinks accommodates both homeowners.

CHEERFUL COLOR (RIGHT)
The right wall color will wake any sleepyhead in the morning. This bath features a vibrant shade of citrus green to liven up the bath and make showering more cheerful.

attic refresher

MORNING WAKE-UP CALL. Attic conversions can be anything but dreary, as this bath aptly illustrates. Distinctive ceiling contours create an alcove suitable for housing the enameled lavastone vanity. Skylights on both sides of the vanity bring in natural light, further brightening the space and showcasing an ornate chandelier. Feel free to use a playful color scheme such as these citrus green walls paired with crisp white wainscoting and bold black and white floral-print fabrics.

PAST AND PRESENT. A reproduction faucet featuring six-pronged handles and porcelain labels references the past, as does the claw-foot tub. More modern conveniences such as the shower and water-saving toilet are cloaked in designs that recollect a bygone era. Built-in shelves next to the vanity are another convenience, eliminating the need for bulky storage.

LIGHT, PLEASE (ABOVE) Brighten a bath with natural light. In an attic where it may not be possible to install windows, consider installing skylights. Here skylights on each side of the vanity provide ambient light.

RETRO REVIVAL (LEFT) This bath pairs modern color choices with distinct period-style features. Faucets and other fixtures are now available in countless shapes and styles.

MAKE SPACE (RIGHT) An attic bath requires creativity when taking advantage of sloped spaces. Shallow shelves installed in a wall recess provide storage next to the sink.

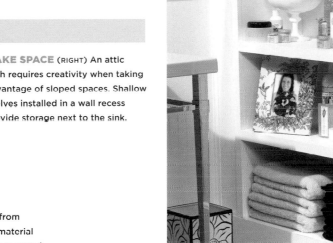

COOL VANITY (BELOW) Made from cooled lava, lavastone is sturdy material for countertops and is easily incorporated into most baths. It comes in a wide range of colors, making it possible to coordinate with bold, colorful designs.

design

Consider your dream bathroom. Will this space be a private retreat for grown-ups only? Something just for kids? A spot for a quick shower or a soothing space to soak away the world's complexities? Use your answers to these questions to create a list of everything you want in your new bath—and don't hold back. This list is an important planning tool. It will ultimately help you determine the size, layout, and furnishings of your bathroom.

master baths

ELEGANT DIVIDER

(ABOVE) A double vanity forms a partition between the tub and grooming spaces in this master suite. To preserve openness the shelves above the vanity create a clear visual connection between sections.

GRAND SCALE. The master bath is often located near or within the master bedroom. Typically conceived on a larger scale than other baths, this space may include an oversize tub, a large walk-in shower, both a toilet and bidet, and a double vanity or two sinks with separate workspaces. Depending on the level of luxury, some master baths even include a whirlpool, dressing rooms, a steam room, and lavish fixtures and furnishings.

SCALED-DOWN OPTIONS. Even if space and budget are tight, a master bath can include luxurious elements. Scratch the steam room and whirlpool tub, but consider including a deluxe showerhead that offers a multitude of spray options. Other ways to save money and space include reducing two sinks to one large unit with double faucets and using laminate and ceramic tile instead of natural stone. Regardless of budget be sure to leave ample space for countertops and mirrors. This ensures both occupants can prepare for the day without stepping on one another's toes.

SHARING SPACES

(BELOW) Although the elevated oval pedestal tub is the centerpiece of this design, the entire room is a harmonious space. One wall is outfitted with separate yet similar grooming areas so occupants can prepare for the day at the same time.

DEGREES OF SEPARATION (ABOVE) Using the proper scale is key for designing large spaces. Here the square mosaic tile soaking tub is the focal point of the room. Double vanities separated by a massive mirror create private grooming spaces. In keeping with the open layout, a high curb contains water in the shower area without closing it off to the room as a shower curtain or walls would.

STYLISH STASHING (ABOVE) Substantial vessel sinks are stylish and they free up plenty of closed storage space below the counter. Combining open and closed shelving ensures quick access to towels while keeping toiletries hidden.

LOCATION, LOCATION (RIGHT) Proximity to the master bedroom is part of a master bath's luxury and comfort. A consistent color scheme and the same flooring material unify these two spaces.

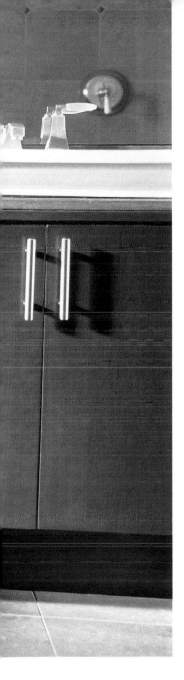

A FLOOD OF LIGHT (RIGHT)
Large spaces benefit from ample light. A bay window brightens this tub area because privacy isn't an issue. Glass blocks high on the wall filter natural light into the enclosed shower area next to the tub.

LOVELY IN LAVENDER (RIGHT)
Situated in front of a large window, the soaking tub is the center of this master suite. Lavender walls, white trimwork, and a checked floor in the same color scheme create a romantic backdrop for soaking away the day's cares.

MADE FOR TWO (ABOVE) No one's bumping elbows in this bath, which boasts two dressing areas and vanities. High ceilings, large linen closets, and an oversize tub are scaled to match the spaciousness of this master suite located in a converted barn.

EASY CHANGE

(RIGHT) A walk-in closet just outside the bath functions as a transition space. The warm, rich tones of the changing room balance the bright bath area.

RELAXING RETREAT

(RIGHT) This master suite includes a sitting area with a fireplace between the bedroom and bath. Similar materials and colors establish continuity between the rooms.

PERIOD DESIGN (ABOVE) These period-style sinks are separated by a tall vanity case, which adds storage space and an intimation of privacy. The recycled pieces of tin ceiling backing the glass-front doors keep the focus on style, not on the towels stored behind them.

TIMELESS DETAILS (LEFT) Large windows flank a vintage hutch outfitted with a sink in this guest bath. The chair—which matches the wood tones in the vanity and mirror—provides a spot for guests to place their luggage or towels.

STOW AWAY (BELOW) Family baths benefit from ample storage. Plenty of undercounter cabinets and drawers combine with a tall freestanding storage unit to stash belongings in this bath.

family & guest baths

CENTERS OF ACTIVITY. Family and guest baths present variations on the same theme. You'll want the same accommodations in each—specifically a space for bathing or showering, grooming, and using the toilet. A guest bath may be smaller than a family bath because it will be used by fewer people, but its amenities should be comfortable.

IN THE ZONES. One of the easiest ways to plan a family bathroom is to create zones that separate different bathing activities as space permits. Half-walls are often better choices than full walls because they tend to cost less to install and provide privacy without blocking light. Plan as much counterspace as you can fit. Multiple vanities, for example, allow family members to get ready for the day simultaneously instead of taking turns in front of one sink and mirror. Make sure each family member has his or her own spot for stashing toiletries.

UP IN THE EAVES
(RIGHT) A family bath
in the attic provides
the perfect location for
a tub tucked beneath
a sloping ceiling.
White beaded-board
wainscoting, a
pedestal sink, and
an antique chest add
vintage charm.

SIMPLE IN STONE (BELOW) Stone floor and wall tiles
create an inviting backdrop for this guest bath. The
green in the tiles is echoed in the accent plants, while
the metal-framed mirror picks up the gray tones.

CORNER COMFORT
(ABOVE) Finding space to
fit everything needed for
a guest bath is a little
easier with simple fixtures.
Outfitting this freestanding
cabinet with a new countertop
and sink costs less than
buying a new vanity.

MARBLE MAGIC (BELOW) High ceilings and a tiled tub surround make this family bath appear spacious. Bullet lights and a minimalist vanity with a vessel sink help create a retreat with Asian flair.

TIGHT AND TIMELESS Even a bath set in a narrow footprint can blend style and function, as this space proves. The dark wood tones of the vanity and tub surround add a welcome contrast to the otherwise bright white room, while lime green serves as an accent color in the towels and rug.

COOL, COMPACT, AND COZY (RIGHT)
Nicely accented with blue floral-print wallpaper, a white and blue color scheme makes this small bathroom seem cozy and bright. A low-profile, low-flush toilet leaves plenty of room for a horizontal shelf, storage, and towel rods.

small baths

SLIM FIT (BELOW)
Installing fixtures in a too-small space may result in an uncomfortable or unusable arrangement. Slim-line fixtures set close together are one way to fit everything.

A LITTLE DOSE OF LUXURY. Bigger doesn't always mean better—as these small baths prove. Although the complexities of daily life increasingly require larger baths to accommodate a multitude of demands, with careful planning even a small bath can feature the right amenities for your needs.

The easiest—and least expensive—way to improve a small bath is to make it look larger than it really is. Consider installing smaller fixtures to free up space. Using light colors, adding mirrors, and removing unnecessary walls are other options for making your small bath appear larger. (See "Small-Space Solutions" on page 53 for more design tricks.)

EXPERT EXPANSION. If you truly need a larger space, and building an all-new bath is out of the question, you may wish to enlarge your current bath. First see if you can steal space from a closet or other area of an adjoining room. Or consider bumping out an exterior wall—you may be able to add as much as 2 feet to your bath without having to add onto your home's foundation.

HIGH AND HORIZONTAL This tiny bathroom looks larger thanks to the horizontal lines of the white subway tile on the walls. Small black accent tiles on the floor extend into the shower, making the shower area seem farther away than it really is.

ATTIC EXTRA (ABOVE) With its thin countertop and slender, wide-set legs, this console sink fits perfectly in an attic alcove.

COUNTER EFFECTS (ABOVE) An extended vanity countertop in a narrow bath focuses the eye on the length of the space—and offers plenty of room for practical activities. A tasteful arrangement of mirrors or other accents emphasizes the long wall and visually enlarges the space.

small-space **solutions**

If enlarging the footprint of a small bathroom is out of the question, try these splashy solutions to alter the perception of its size.

▸ **NEUTRALIZE THE COLOR SCHEME** with pastels, whites, and other soft colors that reflect light and make a room seem larger. Go light on the walls and lighter on the ceiling. Make trim disappear by painting it a shade similar to what is on the walls. Dark colors pull the space together, so save them for accents and interest.

▸ **ACCENTUATE THE HORIZONTAL** with elements such as vanity tops and single shelves. Painted or tiled stripes play tricks with a space, making it seem wider than it really is.

▸ **LIGHTEN UP** by treating windows as the portals of a palace. If you must cover them, use shades that lend privacy without blocking light.

▸ **THINK SMALL** and opt for small tiles on the floor rather than larger units.

▸ **USE MIRRORS** for the biggest impact. Horizontal mirrors appear to double the size of your space. Save the vertical floor-to-ceiling mirror for your bedroom.

ECLECTIC DESIGN (BELOW) With only a corner to spare in this room, everything has to work well together. The modern lines of the sink and faucet look at home paired with the formalities of the faux-stone wall coloring and French Revival mirror.

powder rooms

FRESH AND FANCY. Whether the name originated from the powdered wigs men wore in colonial times or the powdered makeup women wear today, powder rooms provide guests a place to freshen up and are usually outfitted with only a sink and toilet. Although it may receive considerable use, a powder room offers the opportunity to play with design possibilities you may not even consider elsewhere in your home.

LOCATION IS KEY. When located near a rear entry, a powder room provides space for a quick cleanup. In this location it's easy to keep your design purely functional. Placing the powder room near the activity center of a home gives guests and family members a conveniently located bathroom that is easier to access than one located near the bedrooms.

DESIGN DETAILS. Let your imagination fly—special sinks, ornate accents, and bold color schemes may work in your powder room. On the practical side remember to include a window or exhaust fan vented to the outside and be sure to orient the swing of the door to keep the interior of the room private.

HIGHLIGHTS (ABOVE) Create a study in pleasant contrasts by using unexpected materials. Against the textured wallcovering and European design theme, the white pedestal sink is a surprisingly modern accent. The contour of the sink bowl echoes the curve of the antique cabinet.

ANCHORS AND BACKGROUNDS

(ABOVE) Large neutral floor tiles anchor skip-troweled and sponge-painted walls to provide a rich background for the fixtures and accents in this powder room.

RESTORATION OR REAL?
(BELOW) A stylish antique cabinet or hutch base is no less attractive when turned into a vanity with a drop-in sink and nickel-plated faucets.

PERFECTLY PRACTICAL (LEFT)
A powder room or half bath without fancy trappings is comfortably functional as long as simplicity rules.

COACH HOUSE COMFORT (RIGHT)
A long country kitchen worktable serves as a base for a stone bowl sink. Limestone tile on the floor, restoration lantern lights, and period accent pieces emulate the look of an old coach house bath.

NIFTY NICHES Colorful tile niches in the bathing area keep tub toys, towels, washcloths, and soap handy for children and parents. When the kids outgrow the sponge sea creatures, they can use the niches to stash other bathing supplies.

kids' baths

PLAYFUL AND PRACTICAL. Children aren't all business when they're in the bathroom. They look at the bath as another place to play—only this one has water in it. The play may come easily, but when you get right down to it, designing a bath for children can be deceptively difficult. Although you want the bath to fit your child now, you should also consider the future. As children get older, their needs and tastes change, so make certain the style and features of their bath can grow with them.

THEME SCHEMES. If you choose a theme appropriate to your child's age—such as characters from a favorite movie or book—be careful not to go overboard. Use the theme only on items you'll be willing to change in a few years. Faucet handles in the shape of cartoon characters keep things fun, or consider bringing characters into the room through easily replaceable objects such as towels and toothbrush holders.

Wall tiles are a great way to add color—select the right scheme, and the tiles will work for all ages. Or have some fun with paint—if you use bold colors on the wall now, it's easy to repaint later.

THINK SAFE. Because splashing is part of a child's bath process, there's bound to be water on the floor. Choose a waterproof flooring material such as sheet vinyl or vitreous tile with a textured surface to prevent little feet from slipping. (For other precautions to take when planning a bath made for kids, see "Make a Kid-Safe Bath" on page 58.)

SPECIALTY FIXTURES (ABOVE) Some manufacturers carry specialty lines of fixtures for kids. This drop-in sink that depicts a nursery rhyme may be replaced with a more grown-up model when the time comes.

make a kid-safe bath

Before your children splish-splash in the bath, make certain the room is safe for get-clean fun.

- ▶ **SECURE LOWER CABINETS** and drawers using press-release latches, spring latches, or locks.

- ▶ **KEEP THE TOILET SEAT DOWN** with a toilet lid latch.

- ▶ **USE SLIP-RESISTANT MATERIALS** on the floor and traction strips in the tub.

- ▶ **MOVE CLEANING AGENTS** to another room.

- ▶ **KEEP MEDICINES LOCKED** out of reach.

- ▶ **USE PLASTIC**—not glass—tumblers and other accessories.

- ▶ **INSTALL QUICK-ACCESS** privacy locks on doors so you can get in quickly.

- ▶ **PICK UP OBJECTS** left on the floor and countertops, especially those small enough to swallow or that might cause little ones to fall.

- ▶ **KEEP CURLING IRONS,** hair dryers, and electric and blade razors out of reach.

TILT FOR TOTS
(LEFT) Mirrors on swivel mounts allow children to see themselves—like Mom and Dad can.

A QUIET ATTRACTION
(ABOVE) Children's baths don't need elaborate decoration—a simple color scheme may have as much impact. The rounded edges on this sink and tub are an important safety feature, as are no-slip, rubber-backed floor rugs.

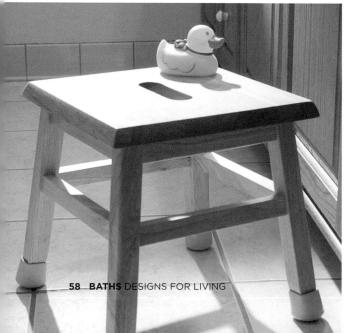

STEP-STOOL SAFETY
(LEFT) Duckies shouldn't be the only rubber objects in a child's bathroom. Rubber feet keep stools from sliding across the floor.

NAUTICAL NOVELTY Although this nautical-theme bathroom goes all out, most of the elements are easy to change should its inhabitants choose to redecorate.

DREAM SUITE (ABOVE) Frosted-glass doors separate shower and toilet areas from the rest of this bath. Added luxuries, including a whirlpool tub, heated towel rack, and custom cabinetry, are artfully integrated in this cool blue space.

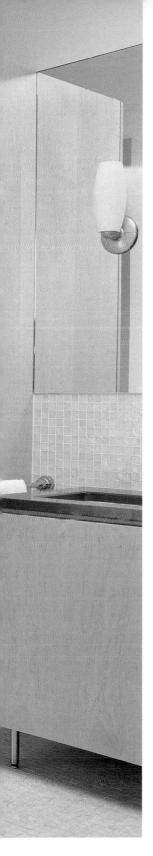

TINTS OF GREEN (ABOVE) For privacy this toilet is separated from the rest of the bathroom. Painting the toilet room the same color as the rest of the bath helped unify the two spaces.

USING RESTRICTIONS (ABOVE) This space's high ceiling, long exterior wall, and plumbing location dictated the spot for the marble shower and platform tub. The light from the windows creates patterns beyond those already in the marble.

best design practices

DESIGN WORKS. Bathrooms are a unique mixture of both practical and aesthetic elements. To create a room that meets your needs, the design should include a well-planned layout styled to reflect your personality and taste.

GOOD DESIGN CHECKLIST. Consider these details during planning.

▸ Arrange the room so the placement of fixtures is related to how much you use them and how much space is available. Also take into consideration the best location for installing plumbing and electricity.

▸ Follow generally accepted guidelines for clearance within the bathroom— particularly around fixtures. These guidelines should be available from your local building department.

▸ Ensure the room is well lit and safe for occupants of all ages.

▸ Include plenty of storage.

▸ Plan for privacy.

A TALL ORDER? With patience, good planning, and some careful attention to detail, all of the elements should come together in a unified design—and you won't be wondering, "Why didn't I think of that?" Because you did.

STUDY IN STYLE

(RIGHT) Black granite and walnut paneling set a dramatic tone as a platform for this tub. Platform surrounds offer a convenient spot from which to enter and exit a tub.

YIN AND YANG (RIGHT)

A half-wall—topped with a shoji screen protected from bathroom humidity by clear plastic—hides a private spot for this toilet.

TUMBLED TREAT

(LEFT) In this tiny bath creative thinking allows everything to fit. A tumbled-stone niche and colorful vessel sink make an intriguing spot for washing up. The wall hides the plumbing.

creating **privacy**

Bathrooms contain public and private spaces. To ensure comfort and style, plan some separation between the two.

In particular create a private toilet area. If it's impossible to locate the toilet in its own room, consider keeping it out of sight by placing it in a nook or behind a half-wall. Transitions between the bath and other areas of the house are important for maintaining privacy too, especially in guest baths and powder rooms. If possible keep the toilet out of direct line of sight by situating it behind a bathroom door. If this isn't an option, it's best if the door opens to a hallway or guest bedroom.

SOLID CONTRASTS

(ABOVE) This dark faucet set stands in stark contrast to the light marble platform surrounding the soaking tub.

STEADY HOLD
(RIGHT) Grab bars are easily included in a new bath or may be retrofitted in an existing one. They should be anchored to the wall framing.

FOR USE BY ALL (BELOW) Slip-proof tiles, single-handle faucets, grab bars anchored to the wall, and a handheld shower unit make this shower safe and easy to use.

accessible baths

EASY ACCESS. Accessibility is an element often taken for granted when designing a bathroom. Whether you have a temporary injury, use a wheelchair, or plan to live in your house well into your golden years, eliminating barriers now is a smart move for the future.

Barrier-free design requires more space, so if you are planning an accessible bath for your current home, you may need to borrow square footage from an adjacent room. Although it may take more work now, incorporating accessibility into your bath ensures it is usable for years to come.

BASIC MODIFICATIONS. Even if completely revamping your bathroom is unlikely, there are steps you can take to ensure that it's easier for anyone to get around.

▸ Install grab bars at toilets, showers, and tubs.
▸ Use lever handles on doors—they're easier to grasp than knobs.
▸ Select slip-proof floors and eliminate changes in elevation.
▸ Widen doorways to a minimum of 32 inches—36 inches is better.
▸ Install faucets toward the front of the sink for easy reach; tub faucets should be accessible from both outside and inside the tub.
▸ Install seating areas in tubs and showers.

UNDER THE COUNTERTOP
Additional space under a sink
makes wheelchair access easier.

universal **design**

Universal design is more than simply a way of meeting accessibility standards. It ensures bathrooms and other spaces function well for everyone.

Universal design is an approach to the design of objects, facilities, and environments intended to make them easy to use by all persons, not just those with disabilities. It advocates that spaces and items within those spaces be accessible to persons with disabilities in a way that does not stigmatize them. After all, large-print labels are easier to read for everyone; public telephones that boost the volume make conversation clearer for all persons; and grab bars in bathrooms make access easier and safer for everybody. Universal design proposes that such improvements be integrated into the design from the beginning of the planning process, avoiding the unattractive and stigmatizing appearance of "accessible" add-ons and afterthoughts.

SAFE AND SECURE A combination of features—a sturdy movable shower seat and slip-resistant floor tiles—ensures this shower is safe and easy to use.

OUTFITTED FOR ACCESS (ABOVE)
An elevated toilet, grab bars near the toilet, extra clearance under the sink, and a swing-out accessory rack make this stylish bathroom accessible for users.

designing for **bathroom safety**

No matter how cautious people try to be, accidents happen. Take additional precautions to ensure your bath is safe for everyone.

- ▶ **STICK** double-faced carpet tape on rugs or use nonstaining antiskid mats to ensure they don't slide on a wet floor.

- ▶ **USE** slip-resistant floor tiles.

- ▶ **MAKE** certain grab bars are anchored to the wall framing.

- ▶ **SET** hair dryers, curling irons, and electric razors on a wide surface away from water sources.

- ▶ **ENSURE** all electric outlets are ground fault circuit interrupter (GFCI) protected.

- ▶ **USE** plastic glasses, soap trays, and other accessories that won't shatter if they hit a hard floor or countertop.

- ▶ **LOWER** the temperature in your water heater to 120°F and install antiscald valves in faucets, tubs, and showers.

SMOOTH MOVES (LEFT)
A safe and smooth transition between the flooring in the bathroom and adjacent rooms is essential for avoiding stumbles and falls.

style

Whether it's contemporary, traditional, old-world, or some eclectic mix, your bathroom should reflect your personality and tastes. Although the baths on the following pages are divided into categories, the real key is to use materials, paint, fabric, furnishings, and accessories to create a style that fully expresses your personality—even if it doesn't fit neatly in a specific stylistic category.

WHITE DELIGHT When the size of the room permits, large-scale furnishings—such as this vanity with furniture-style details—can transform a room. Other elements, including crown molding and marble on the floor, countertops, and tub platform, ensure this design is rooted in traditional style.

TIMELESS TRADITIONAL

(LEFT) In an all-white bathroom, pedestal sinks pair with gold fixtures, ornate frames, and an antique-looking storage piece for timeless style.

traditional

LONG-LASTING. Truly traditional decor never goes out of style—and for good reason. Classic features, such as furniture-style cabinets, ornate molding, and subdued color schemes, might appear formal at times, but they're also key to creating a comfortable, welcoming personal space that is bound to last long after other trends disappear.

CLASSIC DETAILS. Traditional style is characterized by plenty of whites or wood tones—no bold colors here. Although they tend to vary in the details—for instance, some traditional spaces feature undermount sinks, while others showcase ornate pedestal units— common characteristics abound. Carved patterns on furniture, cabinetry, and trim are the norm, as is crown molding and furniture-style detailing.

UNIFYING DETAILS

(RIGHT) Classic design elements, such as a restoration-style plated faucet with matching gold-tone vanity knobs, lend a dose of elegant detail to this bath.

BACK TO BASICS

(RIGHT) Even a simple space can convey traditional style. Here beaded-board panel doors on white cabinets and a pair of fluted mirror frames mimic a classic cottage setting.

COLLABORATIVE ACCENTS (LEFT)

This ample, elegant marble and mahogany bath showcases the luxurious side of traditional design. The vanity, designed with features of an antique breakfront, includes shallow cabinets, inset glass shelves, recessed lights, and crystal and nickel accents.

LAP OF LUXURY (LEFT) Traditional design is far from boring, which this gleaming bath proves. Gold fixtures and knobs pair with an expanse of mirrors and ample lighting to liven up the traditional styling of the white vanity.

design elements

Color, texture, line, and pattern greatly influence the appearance of your bath.

▸ **COLOR** sets the mood for the space— for example, reds and oranges create warmth, while blues and greens are typically soothing hues.

▸ **TEXTURE** is more than tactile—it's also visual. Rough-hewn stone on walls or flooring conveys a rustic appeal, while the smooth lines of marble countertops add a traditional touch.

▸ **LINES** are pivotal in bath composition. Consider how the edges and corners of objects such as sinks, vanities, and windows lend distinction to your composition.

▸ **PATTERNS** can be regular (lending stability to design) or random (creating energy and interest). Choose patterns carefully to avoid overwhelming a space.

PRETTY IN PORCELAIN (LEFT) The intricate legs and exposed plumbing of this wide pedestal sink make it a focal-point fixture. White beaded-board wainscoting furthers the traditional style.

NATURALLY SLEEK (ABOVE) Materials are sometimes used in unconventional ways in contemporary spaces. Here a polished concrete floor glows from the light through floor-to-ceiling windows. Earthy hues of Chinese slate cover the vanity wall opposite a curved wall of textured glass that conceals the shower.

BLACK AND WHITE

(LEFT) White walls, black nonslip rubber flooring, and gleaming fixtures combine to give this bath an urban-contemporary edge. To make efficient use of space, align fixtures on an exterior wall. Here a 7-inch-deep knee wall contains plumbing hookups and provides a ledge for towels.

contemporary

MORE THAN MODERN. Whether you're dreaming of a streamlined, stylish bath characterized by gleaming surfaces or a tranquil, soothing space absent of clutter, contemporary style fits the bill. In these spaces you'll find smooth cabinetry, sleek faucets, and symmetrical arrangements of fixtures and cabinetry. A mix of materials and textures—from stone to metal and glass to exotic wood—combine to create a style characterized by curves in some places and angles in others.

ASIAN INFLUENCES. Some of today's contemporary style is influenced by Asian design. Zen principles based on spiritual stillness and harmony through visual balance are translated into restrained details and minimal, sometimes nonexistent, ornamentation. What is included tends toward the sculptural. Illumination in these spaces comes primarily from natural light and almost invisible fixtures. Muted colors and horizontal lines representing natural elements prevail.

EASY ON THE EYE (ABOVE) Understated earth tones serve as the backdrop for many Asian-inspired baths. In this space the delicate curves of the vessel sink and wallmount faucet offset the straight edges of the vanity counter and glass-enclosed shower.

ALMOST ASIAN (RIGHT) No ordinary porcelain vessel sink, this white bowl reflects a Zen-inspired design. The entire setting, capped by the curved bar supporting the sconces, is a study in the relationships of simple forms, accented by an arrangement of green reeds in the corner vase.

CALMING INFLUENCE (LEFT) Modern materials and graceful forms highlight this bath, which boasts luminescent glass-tile countertops and mahogany cabinets. Polished drawer pulls and a boxy nickel faucet add contemporary touches, as do the vases displayed in the wall niche and on the vanity.

SERENE COMFORT This bath blends natural features and geometric design in a grid of sandblasted translucent windows that back a honey-tone vanity. A sidewall cabinet mimics the design of the vanity windows and helps maintain a clean countertop.

LESS IS MORE (LEFT) An unadorned wooden vanity with a single towel bar sets off a gleaming vessel sink and wallmount faucet affixed to a floor-to-ceiling mirror in this contemporary powder room.

STARTLING OUTLINES Black is an important color in this Japanese composition, especially when used to define such forms as shoji screens and a low platform tub.

NEW OLD-WORLD

(RIGHT) A neutral palette of acid-washed and tumbled marble tile and aged plaster-look walls softens and warms a new bath for a timeworn look.

SUBDUED ESCAPE (ABOVE) Ornate paneling adorns a bathing niche in this elegant space. Other elements fitting with old-world style include a chandelier with crystal prisms, dark wood furnishings, and rich silken window treatments.

surfaces

Surface treatments—the materials on floors, countertops, walls, and ceilings—are the skin of the bathroom. Such elements must endure daily use with grace and charm while supporting the specific style of your bathroom. With material options limited only by your budget, the opportunities for finding the perfect treatment for every surface are almost limitless.

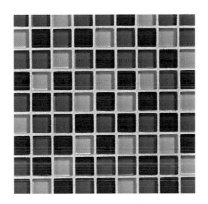

ARTFUL PATTERNS (ABOVE) Granite tile with varying patterns covers the floor and wall in this design, creating strong visual movement enhanced by the contrasting grout color.

flooring

WHAT TO WALK ON. To determine which flooring will work best for you, consider how much use it will get, how it will complement your bath design, and what your budget will allow.

Ceramic and *stone tile* are common bathroom flooring materials because they offer almost endless design possibilities—plus they're durable, water-resistant, and easy to clean.

For baths on a budget, take a look at *laminate* flooring, which provides the look of tile or wood for much less. Laminate stands up to water and wear and is nearly maintenance-free.

Vinyl flooring is another inexpensive alternative available in many attractive patterns. Sheet vinyl may be more practical for baths than vinyl tile because it doesn't have seams through which water can seep and it cleans up easily.

Wood, another bath option, is more susceptible to water damage, so it must be finished with several coats of high-quality polyurethane varnish or paint.

HONED STONE (ABOVE) Honed limestone with lotus-pattern insets provides a neutral base for this old-fashioned pedestal tub. Limestone tiles are porous so they must be sealed to prevent dirt and stain absorption.

PLAYFUL PATTERNS The patterns on the painted floor planks, ceiling, and skylight border in this remodeled attic bath create a playful color scheme. By using the existing wood floor, the owners avoided the cost of a new installation.

WARM FEET (LEFT)
Radiant heat makes almost any flooring material warm and toasty. Electric mats or hydronic systems, which run heated water through plastic pipes, are relatively easy to retrofit under flooring joists. Manufacturer specifications detail which underlayments and flooring materials are suitable for underfloor radiant-heat systems.

selecting **tile**

Picking the proper tile for your bathroom might seem like a daunting task. Approach this decision fearlessly by finding tile that fits these criteria.

▸ **IT DOESN'T SOAK UP WATER.** You'll want vitreous or matte-glazed nonvitreous tile.

▸ **IT STANDS UP TO TRAFFIC.** Tiles are rated for hardness—look for tile with a 7 or 8 rating.

▸ **IT IS SLIP-RESISTANT.** Choose rough-textured tile so the floor is safe even when wet. Save shiny, glazed tile for the walls.

▸ **IT PASSES A TAKE-HOME TEST.** Narrow your choices to three or four types of tile and take samples home for a few days. See how they perform with real-world wear before making your final selection.

RADIANT STONE Polished marble creates an elegant surface for any stately bath. It can be slippery when wet, however, so cover high-traffic areas with slip-proof rugs.

DEFINITIONS (FAR LEFT AND LEFT) Changing patterns and materials or incorporating borders into a design helps define spaces and breaks up large expanses of a floor. Tile is especially suited for this purpose.

LEADING THE EYE (ABOVE) To ensure the oval mirror and sink are the main attraction in this powder room, the diagonal pattern of the black and white tile directs the eye into the room.

STRIKING IMPRESSION (BELOW)
A limestone vanity countertop
with an undermount sink makes
an attractive statement. Because
limestone readily absorbs stains and
dirt, it requires sealing.

DARK IMPACT (BELOW) A
polished black granite countertop
pairs with dark mahogany cabinets.
Granite—particularly dark stone
such as this—is less likely to stain
than other materials.

countertops

COMING OUT ON TOP. Countertops endure almost as much use as flooring. Water, soap, toothpaste, cosmetics, and acetone- and alcohol-based liquids may come into contact with bathroom countertops, so durability is key. In addition to considering how the material will wear, select a countertop that suits the style of your bath.

DESIGN POTENTIAL. Affordably priced *laminate* is the most widely used countertop material. Laminate is available in multiple patterns, colors, and textures; currently stone-look finishes are the most popular. These countertops clean easily and are resistant to water and stains. They can scratch, wear thin, and dull over time, however.

Solid-surfacing, which is typically molded from acrylic resin, requires little maintenance and is more durable than laminate. With solid-surfacing, sinks can be integrated directly into the countertop so there are no seams.

Ceramic tile is dramatic and durable, particularly in moisture-prone areas, and comes in a variety of colors, textures, and shapes. Seal ceramic tile countertops and grout lines to prevent moisture and dirt from penetrating the joints.

EASY FIX (RIGHT) Solid-surface materials can accommodate any style of sink. Dings and scratches easily can be sanded out.

Stone tiles and slabs are classy, versatile, and durable. Slabs are more expensive than tile but eliminate grouting and grout care. Both marble and limestone are porous stones that will stain; proper sealing helps but won't completely eliminate the problem. Granite is less porous and less likely to stain than other types of stone.

UNIQUE CHOICES. Other materials are being put to work on countertops as well. *Natural stones* such as slate and soapstone are durable options that are gaining popularity. *Stainless steel* is seeing more bath duty because of its sleek texture. Copper, brass, and other *metals* are unique options; be sure to seal and care for them appropriately. The dramatic effect of *glass* makes it another popular choice for guest baths or rooms that are used less frequently.

DESIGN CHOICES
(ABOVE) Ceramic tile makes an excellent, durable countertop as long as it's sealed to prevent the growth of mildew.

solid-surface **materials**

Solid-surface materials' ever-expanding design versatility makes them popular for sinks, countertops, and walls. Any of these different styles of solid surfaces may be ideal for your bathroom.

Solid-surface materials are typically cast from an acrylic resin. Because of their chemical composition, these materials are difficult to stain or burn and require little maintenance. Some solvents will soften them, but most damage can be repaired by sanding with fine-grit sandpaper. Solid-surfacing can be used for more than countertops and sinks—the material also comes in panels from $1/4$ to $3/4$ inch thick for wall finishes. A lighter-weight alternative for walls, veneer sheets are $1/8$ inch thick for easier installation. If you opt for veneer, you may have to prep the wall so it's as flat as possible because the material will magnify curves and other malformations.

IT'S GLASS Tempered glass is strong, easy to clean, and stain-resistant. Because it's clear it tends to look like it takes up less space than it does, so it works well in small baths. Glass scratches easily, however, so it's best for baths that are used less frequently.

walls

RUGGED STANDARDS. All materials used in a bathroom must stand up to humidity, clean up easily, and wear well. These standards hold as true for walls and ceilings as for floors and countertops. In addition walls are the largest surface in the bath, so they impact the style of the room.

MANY POSSIBILITIES. *Paint* and *vinyl wallcoverings* are easy, low-commitment ways to achieve finished walls with personality.

Although not recommended for high-moisture areas, *wallpaper* may be used in powder rooms or areas of the bath that are not affected by splashes or condensation.

Ceramic and *natural stone tile* are popular choices because they are attractive and easy to clean. Wall tiles are thinner than floor tiles, so they are slightly less expensive (but not less durable). You can also use heavier floor tiles on walls, but wall tiles cannot be used on floors.

From tongue-and-groove beaded board to polished walnut, *wood paneling* spells quality and permanence. Because wood is subject to water damage, the finish is key.

Glass block transmits light into a bathroom while preserving privacy. It is often used to create interior walls, shower surrounds, and windows.

A CLASSIC MOOD
(ABOVE) Marble walls embellished with columns and borders add a timeless classicism to a bath.

MONOCHROMATIC, NOT MONOTONOUS
(ABOVE) Paint sets the tone for a room as readily as more expensive materials. The lighter band of paint applied just above the middle of the wall adds the right amount of variation to this subdued scheme.

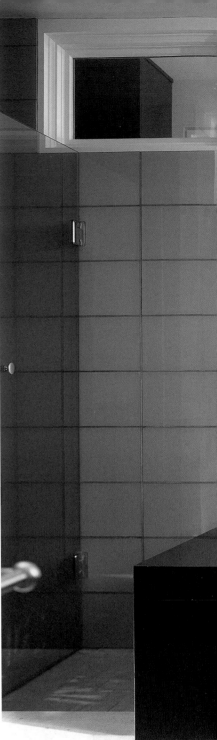

FULL OF LIGHT (LEFT) A glass-block wall and window keep this bathroom feeling bright. Glass block choices range from somewhat transparent to nearly opaque.

NEW BLUE Blue glass tile above a polished black granite tub deck creates a shimmering effect along an entire wall.

TOP TEXTURES (RIGHT) Many techniques exist to add interest to a wall. One of the most easily employed is a tiled accent, such as this handpainted frog. Other effects include stone inserts in a tiled surface and decorative painting, both of which are shown here.

fixtures

Bathroom fixtures—tubs, showers, sinks, faucets, and toilets—are the machinery of the room. These elements will consume the largest chunk of your bathroom budget. You're buying for style, comfort, and longevity, so consider them an investment. Remember that quality and functionality go hand in hand with appearance—no matter how pretty a fixture is, it needs to do the job.

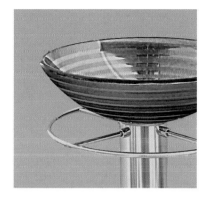

tubs & whirlpools

RECENT INNOVATIONS. The advances made in tub design in recent decades are stunning. Recessed tubs are made to fit within the walls of an alcove; tubs can nestle snugly into corners to save space; and substantial, elegant freestanding units become the focal point of a bathroom. Today most whirlpool tubs come in this multitude of shapes and sizes too.

Before purchasing a tub, sit in it to make sure it fits you and the members of your family. Also determine if it will fit through existing doorways and that it's the proper size for your bathroom.

BACK AGAINST THE WALL (ABOVE) A wallmount faucet is an option when a freestanding tub rests snugly against the wall as this model does.

THERAPEUTIC (LEFT) This soaking tub is deeper than a standard tub, allowing the healthy effects of warm water to cover a bather's entire body. Custom sizes can be installed with custom surfaces.

OLD MEETS NEW (ABOVE) This tub is situated in an alcove to take advantage of stunning views. The tub deck provides a stylish bench, and the step makes it easier to access the tub.

WATER ART (ABOVE) This overflowing tub is set into a trough so water continually flows over the tub edge and recirculates. The result is a soothing sound and an artistic centerpiece for the bathroom.

DROP RIGHT IN (RIGHT)
Installation of a platform-
style tub is versatile because
the tub simply drops into a
separate platform.

MATERIAL CHOICES. The materials from which a tub is constructed will affect its cost, comfort, and durability.

Enameled cast-iron tubs are made from iron molded into a bathtub shape and finished with enamel. Cast iron is thick and durable and retains the heat of the water very well, but it is heavy, so you may need to reinforce the flooring.

Produced by spraying enamel onto molded steel and firing the tub at high temperatures, *enameled steel* is less expensive and lighter weight than iron, but it chips easily and may be noisier when being filled with water.

Acrylic tubs are composed of sheets of acrylic that are heated and formed into a mold, then reinforced with fiberglass and a wood or metal backing. If properly insulated, acrylic tubs hold heat well.

Fiberglass tubs are inexpensive. Their polyester finish is less durable than acrylic, however.

Solid-color polymer-base materials are used to create *cast-polymer* tubs that resemble natural stone. These tubs hold heat well but are less durable than acrylic or enameled cast-iron tubs.

choosing
a whirlpool

A little planning will help you choose the right whirlpool tub, so all you have to do is relax.

Acrylic or fiberglass? Hands down acrylic is the better (but more expensive) choice for a whirlpool tub. It holds heat better and repairs easily, and its color is unlikely to fade. How do you choose the right size tub? Sit in it. You'll quickly discover the best fit. Or if nothing you try feels right, consider having a tile or stone enclosure custom-made to fit your body shape. Next consider water capacity. A 50-gallon model might be too small, but a 500-gallon unit may be too much for your water heater. The configuration of the jets matters too. Large jets mounted on the high sides of the tub gently swirl the surface of the water. Smaller jets farther beneath produce the strongest massage. The key lies in finding what feels right to you.

PROTECTED PLACE
A small tub deck and backsplash protect the walls surrounding this whirlpool tub.

NATURAL DESIGN
(BELOW) A simple freestanding tub resting on oak railroad ties provides a focal point in this bathroom.

HEAVY DUTY (RIGHT)
Tubs constructed of marble or natural stone may require extra bracing so the floor can support the tub.

HIDDEN LUXURY (ABOVE) Although it looks like a standard tub tucked behind a shower curtain, this recessed whirlpool tub features six jets.

EYE ON THE PAST A classic claw-foot tub serves as this room's statuesque centerpiece and evokes the home's gracious Victorian history. Freestanding tubs can be installed virtually anywhere in a room as long as plumbing can be run to the spot.

PRIVILEGED VIEWS This enclosure features a single glass wall on one side to contain splashes, while the rest of the shower is open. A movable showerhead accommodates bathers of any height.

A SPOT FOR TWO (RIGHT) Custom freestanding showers can be fit into any area, but they require labor-intensive installation. This unit is large enough for two bathers and features corner benches that double as storage space.

showers

STALL OPTIONS. Whether you're renovating or building new, modern shower designs present you with numerous choices.

Prefabricated stalls typically are constructed of fiberglass with a finish surface of acrylic or other plastic. They come in one-, two-, or three-piece versions and are designed to fit against a wall or in a corner. The walls of the stall need to be attached to standard wall framing for support.

As an alternative you can purchase *prefabricated shower pans.* They are available in a range of materials from plastic to stone and can be combined with prefabricated shower stalls or custom-made or tiled shower walls.

Custom-made stalls offer the most design flexibility. Any waterproof material from tile to glass block can be used for walls. Only budget limits the size or style of a custom-made shower.

ATTRACTIVE SOLUTION (LEFT) This freestanding claw-foot tub doubles as a shower thanks to a stylish retrofit unit with a showerhead, curtain, and surrounding curtain rod.

OPENLY PRIVATE
(LEFT) A 6-inch rise and a two-sided glass enclosure delineate this shower space from the rest of the room while maintaining a sense of openness. Multiple showerheads and temperature controls provide a spalike experience for one or more bathers.

creating a **steam shower**

Almost nothing beats the luxury of a steam shower in your personal bath—it ranks right up there with a trip to the spa.

To turn your shower stall into a steam shower, equip it with a top and a door that seals tightly. In addition you'll need to install a vapor barrier on the ceiling and wall framing to prevent moisture from causing wood rot. You'll also need to include a steam generator, which heats water from your water system using an electric 220-volt heating element. The necessary size of your steam generator depends on the size of the room and other factors, such as the material covering the shower walls. Check with your supplier to get the correct information.

POOL-HOUSE PATTERN
Simply designed, this mosaic shower and pool-house showerhead create an attractive, uncomplicated space.

LONG REACH An adjustable handheld showerhead mounted on a bar makes it convenient for persons of different heights and can accommodate anyone.

considering
water usage

All showerheads are rated based on flow rate, or the number of gallons of water they spray per minute (gpm).

Although some showerheads still deliver as many as 8 gpms, today's low-flow models deliver just 2.5 gpms and do as good a job of cleaning as the more water-consuming models. Showerhead spray options make a difference too—fine sprays or gentle pulses use less water than coarse or vigorous massage sprays.

RAIN, RAIN, DON'T GO AWAY
(ABOVE) A large rain head makes showering feel like walking in a summer rain, while the lower handheld unit is ideal for rinsing the body.

TOWER OF POWER
(RIGHT) Body spa shower panels like this one are equipped with water jets that pump out and recirculate water for a powerful massage.

showerheads

BEYOND A QUICK RINSE. More and more showers feature a combination of showerheads rather than a single unit, bringing maximum versatility to the showering experience. After deciding how many units you want in your shower, determine which spray heads you desire and the best placement of each.

MOUNTING OPTIONS. Standard *wallmount* units are the most economical option but are the least versatile. You can alter their direction by slightly moving the shower neck. Models that offer a range of sprays are your best bet.

Overhead, or top-mount, units are mounted on the ceiling or the wall or extend from a supporting pipe. Because the spray comes from overhead, it is difficult to avoid getting your hair wet.

Handheld sprayers are now considered standard. In addition to having multiple sprays, these showerheads put the water conveniently where persons of different heights want it and can be used for rinsing the shower enclosure.

Whole-body spray heads produce mists, sprays, and massaging jets at different levels on the wall depending on the model.

sinks

SO MANY CHOICES. Sinks come in many colors, shapes, and particularly materials—including porcelain-enameled cast iron, vitreous china, solid-surfacing, stainless steel, and glass. Consider how much use your sink will get before choosing the perfect model. Less durable, sculptural glass vessel sinks may be best for powder rooms or guest baths that receive less use. In frequently used family baths, larger, deeper porcelain-enameled cast iron may be ideal because it is durable and reduces splashing and countertop cleanup.

BASIC OPTIONS. Bathroom sinks come in three main categories, with variations of each available.

Vanity sinks are the most common and offer the most counterspace. Drop-in models fit into a hole in the countertop so the edges extend over the countertop. Undermount versions attach to the underside of the countertop and require solid, waterproof support. Integral sinks—typically solid-surfacing, stainless steel, or stone—are a seamless part of the countertop. Vessel sinks, which are gaining popularity, are bowls mounted on top of the counter.

Freestanding sinks include pedestals and consoles. Pedestals typically squeeze into small spaces and offer little space for stashing items, while consoles offer some storage below.

Wall-hung sinks are perfect for small baths and powder rooms and are recommended for universal design, but they're usually short on counterspace and storage. In addition plumbing lines are typically visible with these models.

BOLD DESIGN (RIGHT)
Even in basic white a vessel sink makes a dramatic statement. This sink style can be more prone to chipping than others.

SOFT PATINA (RIGHT)
Metal sinks develop a weathered patina that visually warms the room. Paired with a wallmount copper faucet, this sink is at home in a traditional-style bath.

SEAMLESS FEATURE
(LEFT) This glass sink, undermounted in a black granite countertop, pairs contrasting materials to create rugged good looks.

DOUBLE FEATURE Matching vessel sinks on a glass countertop offer space for two yet maintain an airy feel.

GEOMETRIC SHAPES (ABOVE) A white rectangular sink mounted on a black countertop presents a strong geometric line. The sleek wallmount faucet featuring X-shape handles completes the look.

CONTEMPORARY COOL (ABOVE) A custom-made cast-concrete sink with a trough-style bowl sits on custom cabinetry in a decidedly modern bathroom.

installation options

How your bathroom sink is installed depends on the style of sink you select.

▸ **SELF-RIMMING** or surface-mount sinks rest on the top of the counter after the sink is inserted into a hole cut in the countertop. This is the easiest type of installation because the hole does not need to fit the sink exactly. The seam where the rim of the sink meets the countertop is caulked to provide a seal. Consistent cleaning of this joint is important.

▸ **UNDERMOUNT SINKS** are attached to the bottom of the countertop to align precisely with a hole cut in the countertop. This type of installation is more difficult because the hole will remain exposed so it must be cut neatly and accurately. Laminate countertops are not suitable for undermount installation because the countertop material must be waterproof.

▸ **INTEGRAL SINKS** are formed from the same material as the countertop to create one unit with no visible joints. This means that installation involves only the one unit. This easy-to-clean setup provides a sleek look. Any damage to the sink or the countertop, however, means replacing the entire unit.

▸ **VESSEL SINKS** are mounted on top of the countertop or rest partially recessed into a hole cut in the countertop to precise size. Wallmount fixtures are common with this type of sink.

▸ **WALL-HUNG SINKS** typically leave plumbing exposed beneath the sink and are attached to the wall. Fixtures are also mounted to the wall.

▸ **FREESTANDING SINKS**—pedestals and consoles—are supported by a base that rests directly on the floor. Pedestal bases are narrow and lack storage space. Console sinks have two or four legs and may have storage or a towel bar.

FORMAL FLAIR
(ABOVE) Console sink and leg designs tend to favor the ornate flourishes of old. This centerpiece console boasts a brushed-metal faucet that matches the elaborate stand.

VINTAGE CHARM (RIGHT) A white drop-in sink fits perfectly in a black-painted bureau turned into a vanity. The plumbing is hidden behind the cabinet doors.

SLEEK CONTEMPORARY (ABOVE) This tall, single-control faucet in polished chrome boasts minimalist design and a curving handle. It looks at home in a contemporary bath when paired with a shallow, subtly sloping basin and aged-wood countertop.

SUBTLE STYLE (RIGHT) Widespread faucets offer almost unlimited variations in design. This fixture is mounted on the counter.

faucets

IT'S ALL IN THE DETAILS. Faucets are among the details that can spell the difference between a moderately successful bathroom design and a truly remarkable one. But forget about trying to get away with choosing a faucet solely on its looks. Functionality, comfort, and durability are key too. You'll need to make sure the faucet is the proper size and design for your sink before proceeding with installation.

FAUCET PLACEMENT. Most sink and tub faucets mount on the fixture or next to it on the cabinet or tub deck. Wallmount faucets are associated with unusually shaped sinks or other vessels that have been modified for use in a bathroom.

The set of a faucet refers to the configuration of the unit and number of holes needed to mount the faucet. The three basic faucet styles are designed to fit predrilled holes.

A *center-set* faucet has one valve for hot water, one for cold, and a spout. These faucets may have either single-handle or double-handle controls and may be designed for a one-hole or three-hole basin.

A *spread-fit* faucet has separate valves for hot and cold water as well as a spout. The pieces typically have their own holes and are connected below the sink deck.

A *single-handle* set has one valve that controls hot and cold water and a spout in the same unit.

OLD STYLE, NEW VALVE (BELOW) This wallmount faucet sports the look of a vintage fixture—but only on the outside. Inside, a long-lasting cartridge valve controls the water. Cartridges are easy to replace when they wear out. More expensive, but maintenance-free, ceramic disk faucets are also available.

BRASH AND BRASSY
(ABOVE) This polished brass faucet mounted on the sink makes a distinctive design statement.

GRACE UNDER PRESSURE (ABOVE) A brushed chrome finish can convey a sense of antiquity or modernity. Here the curved spout adds a contemporary touch to the design.

SHAPE MAKES A DIFFERENCE (RIGHT) A matte-finish faucet with a modified fluted body creates a composition that looks right at home with this maple backsplash.

VANITY FAIR Spread-fit faucets provide flexibility so the installer can choose (within 10 inches) the amount of space between the handles and spout. These polished brass gooseneck faucets offer greater clearance for washing.

finish **options**

Faucet prices range from $60 to more than $1,000, and it's no surprise that finish options factor into the cost.

Durable chrome is one of the most popular finishes. It is extremely hard, doesn't need protective coating, and is easy to clean. Polished chrome shines like a star, while matte and brushed chrome offer a softer appearance.

Brass is another common finish option. Standard brass finishes are prone to scratching, tarnishing, and corrosion, but new titanium finishes are made to resist these problems. Brass fixtures are commonly available in polished, satin, or antique finishes.

Gold plate in polished, brushed, or matte finishes offers visual appeal. Quality gold won't tarnish, and matte finishes hide scratches. Gold is expensive, however, and the quality of gold fixtures varies. If the finish isn't sealed by a manufacturer, the gold can be damaged.

Other metals, such as nickel, offer visual appeal and durability but can be expensive. You may choose to avoid metals altogether in favor of baked-on enamel or epoxy coatings that are available in many colors and are easy to clean. Just remember that these finishes are prone to chipping or fading over time.

SHINING EXAMPLE
(LEFT) This gooseneck faucet wins style points for its contemporary gleam and X-shape handles.

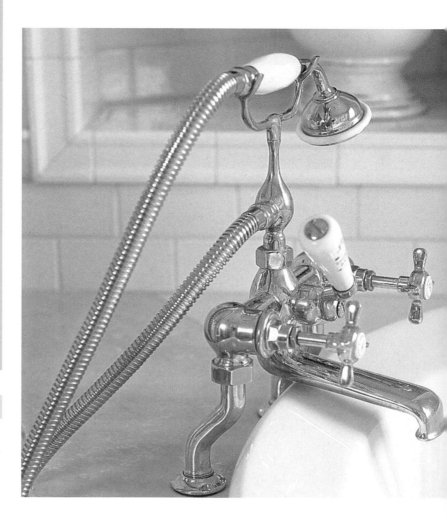

MODERN DELIGHT (RIGHT)
An English-style faucet offers a stationary spout for filling the tub and a convenient handheld sprayer for rinsing.

BRONZE BURNISH Beauty and functionality go hand in hand with the patina of this spread-fit faucet and matching handheld unit.

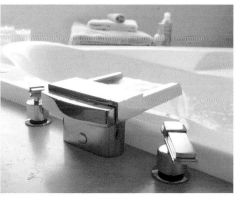

SPOUTING OFF (FAR LEFT AND LEFT) Sink and tub faucets from the same line create a continuity in the design and visually tie the two units together, especially when the faucets are as impressive as these waterfall spouts.

PERFECT MATCH (ABOVE) When a bidet and toilet are placed side-by-side as in this bathroom, at least 15 inches should separate the fixtures. Each fixture takes up at least 3 square feet of floor space.

INDIVIDUAL NEEDS

(ABOVE) Elevated toilets are more comfortable for elderly persons and those using wheelchairs.

TRADE-OFF (ABOVE)

Vacuum-assist and pressure-assisted units are more efficient, but can be noisier than gravity-flush models.

LOW SLUNG (LEFT) Sleek and low slung, a one-piece toilet fits well in a contemporary setting—and saves space in a small area.

toilets & bidets

FUNCTIONAL AND FANCY. From a purely functional standpoint, choosing a toilet is the most important decision you'll make when outfitting your bath. You want comfort, good looks, easy cleaning, and consistent flushing.

One-piece toilets have a lower profile and fewer angles than classic two-piece units. Both styles feature either a round bowl (best for smaller spaces) or an elongated one (most expensive but also more comfortable). Most toilets are available in a multitude of sizes—toilet heights range from the standard 14 inches up to 17 inches—and colors to complement the other fixtures in your bath.

Today's toilets may use no more than 1.6 gallons of water per flush. The least expensive low-flow option is a *gravity-flush* toilet, in which the weight of the water flowing down from the tank clears the bowl. (Read about other low-flow options on page 126.)

BIDETS. Long a popular feature of European baths, the bidet is making headway in American design. Although the fixture resembles a toilet, it looks more like a sink. Water ascends from the center of the bowl to rinse the posterior of the person sitting on the bowl. Unlike a toilet, a bidet requires hot and cold water and a drain. For convenience and to keep expenses down, locate the bidet next to the toilet.

SPACESAVER (ABOVE)
One-piece toilets with round bowls are the perfect choice for small spaces, although elongated bowls are more comfortable.

PAPER, PLEASE (RIGHT)
The best location for the toilet paper dispenser is usually about 8 inches in front of the edge of the toilet bowl.

the latest **on low flush**

Federal requirements mandate that toilets manufactured after January 1994 use no more than 1.6 gallons of water per flush. The first low-flow models were disappointing—many toilets had to be flushed twice, so they saved little water. Fortunately today's low-flow toilets work better than those early models.

In addition to the standard gravity-flush toilet, other more expensive low-flow options are available. The pressure-assist toilet uses pressurized air created from a vessel hidden in the toilet tank to push the water into the bowl and down the drain. Pump-assisted systems, which use an electric pump to propel water into the bowl, are quieter than pressure-assisted toilets and work nearly as well. Use a dual-flush system for a choice between a 1.6-gallon or 8-ounce water flow. Or try a vacuum-assist toilet, which holds water in two plastic tanks and creates increased power for pulling the water down the toilet.

BLACK AND WHITE
The compact white toilet in this guest bathroom boasts a black seat and cover that complement the nearby vanity.

storage

From toiletries to towels, bathrooms tend to accumulate a lot of stuff. Streamline your morning routine and design a space worthy of a soothing evening soak by providing ample storage to corral all of your bathroom necessities. A variety of options—including open shelves, cabinets, drawers, and recessed niches—is the key to developing storage solutions that keep your bath looking and functioning its best.

storage styles

UNDER COVER. Good looks are secondary to function when it comes to bathroom storage. Combine several storage options—including shelves, cabinets, and drawers—to keep personal items tucked out of sight, showcase attractive elements, and ensure that every object in your bathroom is as stylishly stored as it is accessible.

OPEN OR CLOSED? Open storage keeps objects organized but visible. It's perfect for items that you need easy access to and don't mind seeing. Most open storage is in the form of shelves, but a vanity countertop or hooks on the wall are other easy open storage options.

Closed storage keeps things hidden. This is where clutter—including brushes, razors, and hair dryers—goes. Closets, armoires, cabinets, and other objects with doors, drawers, or lids create closed storage. The key is to keep even out-of-sight items organized and readily accessible.

INTERESTING TWIST (ABOVE) Custom vanities allow many storage and design possibilities. The horizontal bars on this vanity provide a spot for hanging towels.

A DIRTY SECRET (RIGHT) Even a wedge of wall offers space to house a built-in hutch for storing clean linens on shelves and dirty ones in drawers.

COOL CUBBIES Extra-deep stone-clad cubbies built into the wall next to a bathroom vanity store rolled towels and decorative objects.

UNFORGETTABLE MIX
A combination of open shelves and closed doors with wooden or glass inserts presents an eyecatching pattern. The shelves without door fronts are ideal for displaying decorative items and stacks of towels.

SIMPLE LUXURY

(RIGHT) An extra-long vanity maintains simplistic order by hiding small appliances and other bathroom necessities in drawers and cabinets.

SMART SOLUTION

(LEFT) A restaurant-style steel shelf unit turns an open wall in a small bathroom into storage for towels and shower supplies. Small items are grouped on trays and in baskets. Pegs screwed into the wall are ideal for hanging robes, towels, or clothing.

5 storage **tricks**

Boost your bathroom's form and function with these storage tips.

▸ **MAKE** cabinets a variety of heights to accommodate family members of different sizes and with different needs.

▸ **USE** pull-down cabinets to meet universal design recommendations.

▸ **CONSIDER** sliding cabinet doors, which may be easier to use because they don't swing out in open space. Pocket doors on closets serve a similar function.

▸ **INSTALL** light-touch and push-and-release catches on cabinet doors to make access easier.

▸ **BUILD** adjustable shelves to accommodate changing storage needs.

EASY REACH (LEFT)
Towels draped over a tilted ladder fill dead wall space. They dry faster if hung rather than folded.

bathing

GOOD & CLEAN. The accoutrements of bathing are many—towels, shampoos, soaps, sponges, and lotions all are necessities that must be kept close at hand. But where do you stash all of this stuff so it's easily accessible for carefree bathing?

Identify where you'll most often use bathing booty. It makes sense to store shampoos, conditioners, and soaps in the shower or beside the bath. A towel and washcloth for each occupant should be within easy reach too. But extra towels, lotions, and specialty items are best kept a few steps away from the action, where they're still accessible but out of the way.

STORAGE STRATEGIES. Open storage is your best bet for stashing objects that are regularly used in or near the tub or shower so you can avoid opening doors or pulling on drawers with wet hands. Away from the bathing areas, almost anything goes. Towels may be stacked, rolled, or hung. Other items may be lined up on shelves, hidden in drawers, or stashed in baskets. Play around with storage combinations to discover what works best for you.

NICE VIEW (LEFT)
Glass inserts in cabinet doors allow views of stacked towels and stylish containers of salts and soaps.

SECRET STORAGE

(LEFT) A wallmount window seat pulls double duty with a flip-down door that hides towels.

HOLE IN THE WALL

(BELOW) A tiled bath niche is more than a practical spot for stashing shampoo and conditioner. It's also a stylish way to continue a bath's color scheme.

HELPFUL SHELF (ABOVE) Backsplash units work well in the bathroom. This chrome-plated shelf is perfect for holding wet washcloths and keeping hand towels within reach.

IN THE CLOSET Fabric-lined baskets tucked away in a closet offer accessibility and partially conceal their contents.

the best cabinetry **for your bath**

So you've decided you want built-in cabinetry rather than portable storage. Hold on—you still have work to do. Here are some clues to figuring out which type of cabinetry best suits your style, needs, and budget.

A relatively inexpensive choice, stock cabinets are the ready-to-wear equivalent of cabinetry. They come off the production line in standard sizes, finishes, and styles. Although stock cabinetry may boast good finishes and fine quality, the range of accessories can be limited. Move a step up to semicustom cabinets and you'll find slightly better materials and more design flexibility. Expect to pay a bit more and wait longer for the product to be completed, however. As you might expect, custom cabinetry is the most expensive but also the highest quality option. Cabinetmakers construct the cabinetry to meet specific needs, fit special spaces, solve unusual layout problems, or create new designs.

grooming

GETTING PRETTY. No matter your
gender, grooming involves more than
running a comb through your hair.
So storing grooming items tends to
encompass more than a single drawer
in the bathroom. In fact sometimes
prepping and primping demand a
whole section of the bathroom. Whether
your grooming area is contained to the
countertop beside the sink or spread
out in a separate area defined just for
that purpose, everything from razors to
cotton swabs should have a place.

STORAGE STRATEGIES. If counterspace
is plentiful keep it organized by grouping
supplies on serving trays. When a spot
on the counter is at a premium—perhaps
because you share one sink and mirror
with someone else as you get ready
for the day—it's best to stash personal
toiletries away from the vanity but within
easy reach. Double vanities allow occupants
to store items in their personal areas
rather than sharing storage. No matter
which storage option you choose, consider
how items will look. Hide clutter behind
closed doors or display small objects in
jars or baskets if they're out in the open.

BRIGHT IDEA (LEFT)
Thoughtfully placed
in front of rows of
windows, this makeup
table takes advantage
of brilliant natural light.
Drawers hide some
items, while others are
smartly displayed on a
tray on the countertop.

TIGHT SQUEEZE (ABOVE) Storage abounds
at this vanity with two sinks separated by a
lower counter. Each side of the vanity features
undercounter storage and wall-hung cupboards.
A drawer beneath the makeup counter stores
smaller items.

materials
and finishes

**At first glance, stock
and semicustom cabinetry
may look the same. Yet closer
examination often reveals large
differences in the quality of
materials and construction.**

**With cabinetry you really do get
what you pay for. Particleboard is a
common material for stock cabinet
cases, especially those covered with
laminates and vinyl finishes. You'll
often find a stronger product, medium-
density fiberboard (MDF), in midpriced
lines. For the best in long-lasting,
durable cabinetry, look for units made
with heavy-gauge plywood cases,
substantial and solid door and drawer
construction, and heavy, smoothly
rolling drawer glides. Laminates and
veneers are commonly used to surface
cabinets. You'll pay more for high-
pressure laminates or thick veneers
coated with a multistep polyurethane
varnish process, but over time it will be
worth the expense.**

ASIAN CONTRASTS (ABOVE) This vanity imports a hint of the Far East while providing ample storage space in a narrow bath. Dark wood cabinetry with geometric door and drawer pulls opens to reveal storage for two. White vessels on the black granite countertop hold toiletries used on a regular basis.

RAISING THE BAR (ABOVE) When undersink storage is out in the open, practicalities such as cleaning supplies must be tucked away elsewhere. Metal canisters provide stylish undervanity storage in this bathroom.

ON DISPLAY (LEFT) Because counterspace is plentiful in this bathroom, toiletries grouped on high-style serving items make a pretty arrangement.

shelves

SHALLOW THINKING. The functional advantage of shelving is that while it stores things, it takes up no floor space. In a bathroom, shallow shelving may be all that is necessary because bathing and grooming items are often small. The trick in designing shelves of any size is to make certain they're not too deep, so what you want to find is within reach. If small items end up looking cluttered on your shelving, organize similar objects in containers such as baskets or bins and place the containers on the shelves.

SHELF STRATEGY. Shelves have a tendency to end up anywhere on the wall, but the best place for often-used items is where they are most accessible— between knee and chin level. This eliminates the need to reach too far up or down. If display space is what you need, hang shelving anywhere 18 inches or so below the ceiling.

COZY CUBES (ABOVE) An attractive alternative to typical wall-hung shelving, cubes can be purchased in separate units or as a one-piece cabinet. Cubes stacked to various heights provide an interesting visual element and a creative use of vertical space.

WARM WELCOME
(LEFT) The warm wood tones of this tall corner cabinet match those of the mirror frame and vanity base. When a vanity doesn't include undercounter storage, placing a cabinet nearby provides a spot for bathroom necessities large and small.

fighting **grime**

Bathrooms—particularly countertops and cabinetry—get messy. Prevent your bath from falling victim to spills, water damage, and humidity by keeping these points in mind.

The more elaborate your cabinetry molding is, the harder it will be to clean. Cabinets that boast flat doors with a baked-on finish are easiest to wipe down. Stained cabinets with a flat or no-gloss finish don't show dirt as well, but they are easily marred and harder to touch up. Remember to consider cabinet hardware too—pulls and handles that prevent the cabinet surface from getting dirty work best. If you organize potentially messy items such as toothpaste and lipstick tubes in drawers, install acrylic liners that can be removed and washed when soiled.

NO SPACE WASTED (LEFT)
Half-walls that are built for
privacy make good storage
spaces too. If medicines and
other hazardous products
are stored in a low, recessed
cabinet, a lock should be
installed so young children
cannot access the contents.

medicine cabinets

MORE THAN MEDICINE. Medicine
cabinets are key for storing small items
above or near the vanity. In addition to
stashing cosmetics or toothpaste, these
cabinets often are used to keep medicines
and other hazardous objects high so they
are out of reach of small children. Most
medicine cabinets come with mirrors
and are hung directly above the sink.
For variety in your bathroom design,
consider locating the cabinet on a
sidewall or elsewhere in the room—above
the toilet, for example—and leave the
space above the sink for mirrors.

VARIATIONS. Most medicine cabinets
are surface mounted, which means they
extend from the wall and take up the space
in front of it. In a bathroom makeover
you have the chance to recess the
cabinet within the walls, which frees
up space. No matter where you mount
the medicine cabinet, consider one
with stair-step shelves, which make
organizing and accessing items easier.

MIRROR-FREE
(ABOVE) Fluted glass gives a stylish look where a mirror might go.

SPACE-AGE STYLE (ABOVE)
In this contemporary bath a circular mirror pivots to reveal the medicine cabinet behind it. In a small space a cabinet with a couple of simple shelves may be all that fits.

PLEASANT TOUCH (LEFT)
Blackboard paint inside a medicine cabinet door provides a message board for morning niceties.

COOL BLUE Common bathroom accessories include towel hooks and a scale. A carafe and glass for drinking water and a petite silver vase for showcasing fresh cuttings are personal touches in this bath.

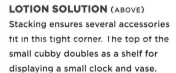

BRIGHT WHITE
(LEFT) An all-white bath with coordinating accessories is consistent with fresh country style.

LOTION SOLUTION (ABOVE) Stacking ensures several accessories fit in this tight corner. The top of the small cubby doubles as a shelf for displaying a small clock and vase.

accessories

SMART ADDITIONS. Small decorative touches—a sleek soap dish, a well-placed towel bar or robe hook, and a wastebasket—are key for creating a finished look in any bathroom. The variety of choices available for outfitting your bath, from toothbrush holders and tissue dispensers to vases and potted plants, proves that the details play a major functional and decorative role in establishing a bath you can truly use and enjoy.

STAY IN STYLE. Before you go shopping identify which accessories are necessary for your bath. There's no need to purchase a soap dispenser, for instance, if you already have a dish on the sink that matches your decor. The style of the accessories matters too. An eclectic mix of objects might work in a bath with unfitted cabinetry and old-world styling, but in a contemporary space a set of matching streamlined items may better complement your bathroom design.

CLASSIC TOUCH (ABOVE) A bath caddy with multiple compartments spans the tub, so soap, brushes, and a loofah are easily accessible to the bather. The accessories coordinate with other elements in the space, such as the English-style faucet.

PRACTICAL PULL
(LEFT) Cabinet pulls should match door and drawer styles. Sleek pulls work with full overlay drawers, crystal knobs dress up classic styles, and bin pulls coordinate with natural wood tones.

CONTEMPORARY FORMS
(RIGHT) The rounded form
of these pulls is in contrast
to the gridlike pattern
established by the drawers.

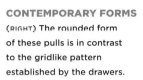

STREAMLINED STYLE
(ABOVE) Stainless-steel pulls
create strong horizontal
and vertical lines typical of
contemporary design and
make it easy to open doors
and drawers.

hardware

MAJOR PULL. Once you select a cabinet style, turn your attention to drawer pulls and door handles. More than mere functional necessities, cabinet hardware contributes to the overall impact of a bathroom's design.

No particular rules apply for selecting the right hardware. Personal taste may guide your selection, but consider how the hardware will function as well as how it will work with the rest of the room. Regardless of the style of hardware, for accessibility choose knobs or handles that are easy to grasp and pull. If you are emulating Shaker style with flat-panel cabinet doors, simple brass knobs may do the trick. If you're creating a contemporary space, sleek pulls in brushed chrome or stainless steel might fit better.

THINK HINGES. Although not visible like drawer pulls or knobs, the right hinges are key to ensuring doors fit properly on the cabinets. Any part of the hinge that shows should complement the rest of the hardware. Inset doors are best mounted with hinges on the inside surface or with butt or wraparound hinges. Rabbeted doors are usually installed with lipped hinges. Overlay doors are made to be outfitted with invisible hinges.

lighting & climate

Proper bathroom lighting provides shadowless, glare-free illumination throughout the room—so everything from showering to applying makeup is easier on the eye. Beyond ambient and task lighting, incorporating natural light from skylights or windows creates an inviting retreat. For a truly comfortable space, use the right heating sources and ventilation techniques as well.

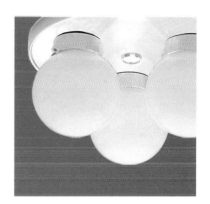

NATURAL LIGHT
(LEFT) A window or
skylight brightens up
a dark bathroom by
ushering in the sun,
which is an important
source of ambient light.

lighting design

CASTING LIGHTS. Good lighting design should not only illuminate the vanity area. It should make the bathroom safe, cast light in each functional area, and create the overall ambience you want. Plan for a blend of at least two of the three main illumination strategies: ambient, task, and accent lighting. When possible, good lighting design also includes natural light from windows or skylights.

Ambient lighting, which is also called general lighting, creates a uniform, overall glow in the entire bathroom and usually comes from one or more overhead sources.

Task lighting illuminates a specific area such as the mirror, the vanity, and perhaps the tub and shower. Use wallmount sconces, pendent lights, track lights, or light bars for task lighting.

Accent lighting highlights decorative objects or forms. Consider using toe-kick lights, wall sconces, low-watt halogen lights, or recessed lights to accent certain areas in your bath.

LIGHT TEAM (ABOVE) Surface-mount ceiling lights illuminate this room, while modern sconces affixed to the mirror provide task lighting. Generally ambient lighting requires 75 watts of fluorescent light for every 50 square feet of floor space.

BRIGHT AND WARM (RIGHT) White-glass sconces with polished-nickel bases serve as task lighting around a mirror, blending contemporary lines and traditional warmth. Task lighting should provide 40 to 50 watts of fluorescent light.

ART DECO ELEMENTS (LEFT) Overhead task lighting illuminates each sink in this master bath, but the handcrafted lighting fixture made from antique glass is what draws attention to the vanity area.

DOWNCAST (BELOW) Compact fluorescent bulbs work well for task lighting placed above a vanity mirror. The frosted and fluted globes on this bar light provide illumination without creating glare on the mirror.

UNUSUAL TWIST
(LEFT) Placing clear
incandescent lightbulbs
in caged outdoor
fixtures provides
contemporary task
lighting above these
individual mirrors.

extending
your design
with **mirrors**

**Mirrors perform multiple
functions and require only an
expanse of wall space.**

Mirrors can extend and reinforce both
the lighting and general tone of your
bathroom. A mirror's size, shape, and
frame contribute to the bathroom's
ambience. In addition to providing a
spot for checking your appearance,
mirrors help visually enlarge small
spaces. Mirrors also reflect and
redistribute light throughout the room,
whether it's natural light streaming in
through windows or general and task
lighting from artificial sources.

SUBTLE AMBIENCE Because this bathroom mirror serves as the primary grooming center, it is evenly illuminated with recessed lighting above the mirror as well as task lighting in the form of a lamp on the vanity countertop.

bulb **options**

The one-size-fits-all days of the incandescent bulb are long gone. Today's bulbs come in sizes, shapes, and types for every conceivable purpose.

▶ **INCANDESCENT BULBS**, the standard for decades, are still widely used and are available in frosted and clear styles and a wide range of wattages. Today's bulbs are more energy efficient and longer lasting than the incandescents of the past. Low-voltage incandescent fixtures make good accent lighting.

▶ **FLUORESCENT LIGHT**, once available only in tubes that flickered and made noise, now comes in a compact energy-efficient alternative for incandescent lights. You'll also find fluorescent circles and rope lights for cabinet and cove lighting.

▶ **HALOGEN LIGHTS** offer bright white light good for task or accent lighting. Even low-voltage halogens produce a large amount of heat, so choose fixtures specifically designed for them.

BLOCK PARTY (LEFT) A wall of glass block ushers in light and provides ambient lighting for pedestal sinks and mirrors. A single pendent light creates task lighting and enhances the sculptural composition of the space.

light fixtures

MOOD MAKERS. Bare bulbs create light, but it takes lighting fixtures to create mood, ambience, and focus. No one type of bulb or fixture can do all your lighting—you'll likely need a combination of styles to fully illuminate your bath.

Recessed downlights, also called can lights, are popular fixtures for general or task lighting. These fixtures are set into the ceiling and cast light down either straight or at an angle, depending on their style. Use them for general lighting and to fill in areas where task lighting leaves shadows. Overlap the spread of recessed downlights' lighting patterns for continuous coverage.

Pendent fixtures hang from the ceiling on a chain, wire, cord, or metal rod. Use them for general or task lighting. Pendent fixtures come in various styles. Even a single pendent or small chandelier can create an impact.

Surface-mount fixtures, such as sconces on walls or track lights on ceilings, work well in spaces that cannot accommodate recessed fixtures.

Shower fixtures must be waterproof and steamproof, a requirement of most building codes.

DOUBLED UP (RIGHT) The translucent frosted shades on this double sconce look best lit with incandescent bulbs.

CLASS ELEMENTS (RIGHT) A suspended fixture creates indirect general illumination by reflecting light up to the ceiling and diffusing it throughout the room.

WINDOW TREATS
(LEFT) Where window placement raises privacy issues, blinds that match the style of the bath let in light while maintaining privacy.

PRACTICAL PLACEMENT (LEFT) Windows placed in a toilet area should be high enough on the wall to provide privacy or should include coverings such as these shutters. Operable windows will provide extra ventilation.

windows

NATURAL ILLUMINATION. A good bathroom lighting plan should include as many ways of bringing in natural light as possible. Window styles and placement are key to creating a visually pleasing bath that ushers in natural light but still preserves privacy.

The proportions and features of your room should dictate window size—for instance, a window intended to accent a tub should be large enough to light the tub's width. Look for places to install windows that will shed more light on the vanity area without looking out of place with your home's exterior. And don't be afraid to mix and match window styles—a bay window might look best in front of a tub, while double-hung windows may be useful additions to a sink or toilet area.

LIGHT SPREAD Plenty of light and warmth issue through these large triple-glazed windows. The insulating value of these energy-efficient windows keeps the inside surface warm and prevents condensation on the glass on cold mornings.

ONE WITH NATURE
If views are prime and privacy isn't an issue, a soaking tub surrounded with windows provides enjoyment of the outdoors while bathing.

BRIGHT IDEA (RIGHT) Glass block provides the glow of natural light without the view, which makes it ideal for a shower wall. Proper ventilation is required, however, so the glass block resists condensation.

selecting **windows**

Look for energy-efficient double- or triple-glazed windows in a style that complements your home inside and out.

Refined materials and improved details mean today's window selection is more expansive than ever. A safe bet is the traditional design of single- or double-hung windows. Double-hung styles employ two sashes that slide up and down within the frame. Only the lower sash is operative on single-hung models. Casement windows pivot on hinges, with their outward swing controlled by a hand-crank mechanism attached to the windowsill. With gliding windows one or two sashes slide horizontally in the tracks of a frame. To maximize views select picture windows, which are stationary windows used for light and views only. Or try any of the many specialty windows available today—including round, half-round, and other nonstandard configurations.

SHEER LIGHT (ABOVE) Semisheer window treatments let in light while maintaining privacy.

ORGANIC STYLE A frameless glass wall separates a shower wall from a private atrium in this master bath. Rustic wooden-beam skylights overhead provide additional illumination.

WHITE LIGHT (ABOVE) White frames help the skylights in this traditional white bathroom blend with the decor, so the only thing occupants notice is the profusion of natural light.

skylights

LET THE SUN SHINE IN. If wall space is limited or views are less than appealing, consider installing a skylight in your bathroom. Skylights can be purchased with frames that match wall windows for consistent style. Today's models, if properly installed, are virtually leakproof. Many models are now made to open either manually or with motorized systems, so they offer ventilation as well as natural light.

ATTIC SOLUTIONS (RIGHT) A skylight casts ample light on this attic shower stall. Skylights are an especially effective medium for bringing natural light to attic baths.

ADDED LUXURY (LEFT) Towel warmers are either electric or hydronic units. Hydronic heaters warm towels by circulating either hot water or steam inside brass tubes. They are usually less expensive and heat more quickly than electric ones.

venting & heating

FRESH AIR Without proper ventilation everything from the tub fixtures to the walls may begin to deteriorate. Where possible install operable windows and doors to add ventilation throughout a bath.

AIRFLOW IDEAS. Everyone knows that bathrooms get steamy and wet. Without proper ventilation, humid conditions can lead to mold and mildew. When computing the ventilation requirements for a new bath, take into account the size of the room and the number and placement of windows. Although windows are a great source of ventilation, every bathroom is well served by a ventilation fan. In fact many local building codes require exhaust fans in new bathroom construction. A system that moves all of the air from the bath to the outdoors is recommended.

WARM THINGS UP. Electric heaters made for mounting on walls or ceilings or under toe-kicks are easy add-ons. Models are available for use with gas or propane heat as well.

Another option is radiant heat, which warms a space more evenly than other systems. Pipes or electric mats can even be added under most flooring materials to keep feet warm.

Also consider spot sources of heat, such as infrared heat lamps and electric towel warmers, which won't heat entire areas but will add a level of comfort to your bath.

BATHTIME FAN (ABOVE)
If your bath is sealed tight, a
ventilation fan can't do its job.
If possible open a window after
you take a shower to help the
fan draw in fresh air.

SMART HEAT (ABOVE)
Solar panels and radiant
heating units under this
travertine tile floor warm
bare feet and increase the
overall temperature of the
room. Like other heating
systems, underfloor
heating is controlled by
a thermostat that can
be adjusted.

choosing **an exhaust fan**

Ventilation is an important part of bathroom design—in fact, it's
mandated in codes for new construction and even for renovations in
some areas. Three criteria matter when choosing a ventilation fan.

▶ **HOW MUCH AIR THE FAN MOVES.** A vent fan should move the air in your
bathroom from inside to out eight times an hour. Fans are rated by how
many cubic feet per minute (cfm) they can move. To calculate your bath's
cfm requirement, take the square footage of your bath and add 5 to it.
A 100-square-foot bath would need a fan rated at 105 cfm or higher.

▶ **HOW MUCH NOISE THE FAN MAKES.** Sound is rated in sones. A higher rating
means the fan is louder. One sone generates about the same noise as a
refrigerator, so you'll probably want to look for a fan that produces less than
3 sones at full speed.

▶ **HOW THE VENT LOOKS WITH THE REST OF YOUR STYLE.** Once the specifics
of fan size, efficiency, and sound are considered, choose a vent style that
best matches the rest of the room.

luxury

Baths are more than places for bathing and grooming—many of them are downright luxurious. Sink yourself into these lovely spaces brimming with lavish textures and fixtures as well as the best in spalike amenities, including fireplaces and saunas. You may discover that one of these spaces is exactly what you need to create luxury in your own home.

 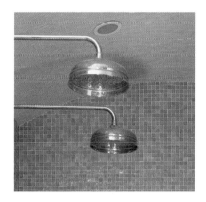 

SPECTACULAR SKYLINE (ABOVE) Resembling a window seat, this whirlpool tub is placed to take advantage of the room's breathtaking view. A large tub surround and nearby bench ensure all of the luxuries of bathing are within arm's reach.

BY CANDLELIGHT (RIGHT) Candles near the tub establish a relaxing mood in this bath.

pampering retreats

**SPA DETAILS** (BELOW) Plush cotton towels, soothing bath oils, natural sponges, and fresh flowers are details that make bathing a pleasurable experience.

SWEET SETUP. Each person's ideas of pampering may be different—one might be after a space that's simple and streamlined with an emphasis on the most important physical comforts; another may wish to go all out with every amenity and indulgence imaginable. It's all a matter of preference and, of course, budget.

Anything goes when creating a completely luxurious bathing retreat. But be sure to think about incorporating some general features into your design. A truly luxurious bathroom is one that's pleasing to the eye. Ample windows, accent lighting, and mirrors brighten the space while maintaining a soothing atmosphere. A muted color scheme induces instant relaxation. Towels and robes are soft and fluffy. And added amenities—perhaps radiant heat flooring, towel warmers, and an expansive whirlpool tub—ensure that every trip to the bathroom is as wonderful as can be.

HIDDEN LUXURIES (ABOVE)
You could almost stay forever in a master suite that includes amenities such as a coffee bar or refrigerator. This custom-made armoire hides electronics and a small refrigerator.

IT'S IN THE DETAILS (ABOVE)
A small decorative niche in the shower to store spalike elements such as bath salts is an artistic touch that further personalizes the bathing experience.

at-home spa experience

Beyond the whirlpool tub, for a resort experience at home you may want to include these extra amenities.

MUSIC. Add miniature speakers on shelves or in cabinets to fill your room with soothing music from your home stereo system.

SOAPS AND OILS. Infuse your bath with your favorite scents. Have a selection of invigorating and relaxing fragrances on hand to cater to your mood.

WARMTH. Warm your feet with thick, toe-tickling rugs and wrap yourself in an oversize towel like those in a luxury hotel. To provide toasty towels consider adding a towel-warming bar to your bathroom.

FLOWERS. Arrange bouquets of fresh flowers on countertops or windowsills to instantly brighten your bath.

A TOUCH OF HISTORY
(BELOW) A claw-foot tub paired with gleaming gold fixtures, period-style sconces, and mahogany vanities lends this master bath the ambience of an 18th-century dressing suite.

FOR SIMPLICITY'S SAKE (ABOVE) Sometimes sleek simplicity is all that's required to create a soothing space. The muted tones of this bath encourage relaxation, as does a clutter-free vanity highlighted by a sculptural wallmount faucet, a potted orchid, and plush towels.

SUPER SHOWER (RIGHT)
In a creative interpretation of spa style, this steam shower boasts blue glass mosaic tile walls, two large showerheads with exposed valves, and a 6-foot-long bench as a nod to old gyms and locker rooms.

MODERN ELEGANCE (BELOW)
Emulating 1920s design this new bath includes honed Italian marble countertops and generous mahogany woodwork. A built-in bookcase near the tub allows for watching television while soaking.

INVITING ESCAPE
(ABOVE) This well-appointed bath is made for indulgence with a dramatic blue chaise situated in front of the tub.

ASIAN AESTHETIC
Asian-inspired design,
a private glass-walled
bathing area, and ample
natural light make this
space a serene retreat.

TWO'S COMPANY Back-to-back vanities in the middle of the room make this spacious bath a cozy retreat for two. The placement frees up wall space for work centers including a makeup vanity, built-in storage armoire, shower for two, and freestanding soaking tub with remote-controlled jets.

kitchen design ideas **in the bath**

Take a cue from hardworking kitchen designs to create a master bath loaded with luxurious yet practical amenities.

To make the best use of a large master bath, consider laying out the room more like a hardworking kitchen than a basic bathroom. Just as an island breaks up the space and creates a work core in a kitchen, this bath's back-to-back vanities (*above*)—each equipped with a sink, counterspace, and two banks of drawers—are located in the center of the room. This leaves wall space for function-packed centers much like the work centers in a well-designed kitchen. For instance, a built-in armoire includes a warming drawer for heating towels. A coffee bar complete with a sink and undercounter refrigerator allows the homeowners to grab a cup of coffee or a snack during morning grooming time.

SECLUDED SOAKS (RIGHT) A whirlpool tub situated away from the rest of the bathroom truly captures a spa feel. Temperature and lighting controls located near the tub allow occupants to adjust the heat and illumination of the bathroom accordingly.

OPEN ACCESS (RIGHT) A small private patio just outside the bath extends a private retreat into the backyard, providing a spot for relaxing outdoors after a bath or shower.

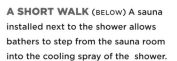

JUST THE BASICS
(RIGHT) Saunas require little floor space—even a small 4×4-foot closet provides enough space for a sauna heater and a bench.

A SHORT WALK (BELOW) A sauna installed next to the shower allows bathers to step from the sauna room into the cooling spray of the shower.

saunas & steam rooms

HOME SPA. Although the health benefits of saunas and steam rooms have been known for centuries, these luxurious amenities are still gaining popularity. This is, in part, a result of the ingenuity of American manufacturers that have created sauna and steam room kits that can be installed in almost any bathroom.

KIT OR CUSTOM? If you have about 16 square feet to spare (about the size of a small closet), you can have your sauna or steam room built to order or you can build it yourself with a prefabricated or custom kit. Prefab units are sold only in specific sizes, while custom kits allow you to provide measurements to a manufacturer that cuts the materials to size. Style is important, however, so if you're looking for a sauna or steam room that perfectly matches the style of your bath, you may wish to contact a local contractor to custom-build one for you.

STEAMY ELEMENTS (ABOVE)
Iridescent glass tiles and variegated slate line the walls of this steam room, which doubles as a resort-quality guest bath.

RELAXATION STATION (RIGHT)
Even on sunny days a fireplace adds ambience to a tub area. This tiled fireplace surround matches the backsplash along the wall, creating continuity in the bath.

TREAT FOR THE EYES (BELOW) Decorative painting adorns the elaborate fireplace and tub surrounds in this bathroom, creating a rich old-world retreat.

fireplaces

THE ULTIMATE AMENITY. Soaking in a whirlpool tub in front of a fireplace is no longer a luxury reserved solely for spa outings. Increasingly homeowners are including fireplaces in their bathrooms for the warm mood they create.

A fireplace may be built on a flat wall or in a corner of the room with materials that match your bathroom style. Many are installed in a wall between the bedroom and bathroom so both spaces benefit from the fireplace.

Although they are still used occasionally, wood-burning fireplaces are less common in bathrooms than gas or electric ones. Regardless which type of fireplace you choose, installation is best planned from the start of a bathroom project and should be handled by an expert so that proper ventilation and safety precautions are taken.

DOUBLY DELUXE (ABOVE) A two-sided
gas fireplace breaks up the wall between this
bathroom and the adjacent bedroom, warming
both spaces.

contact
information

The Home Depot® offers bath products and materials from major manufacturers either in stock or through special order. This extensive inventory offers you a comprehensive and varied selection that will ensure a bathroom that truly reflects your style while enabling you to stick to your budget. Because The Home Depot constantly updates its inventory to bring you innovative products and materials, the best source of information on what is currently available can be obtained from The Home Depot associates at your local store or online at www.homedepot.com.

Contacting Meredith Corporation

To order this and other Meredith Corporation books call 800/678-8091. For further information about the information contained in this book, please contact the manufacturers listed or contact Meredith by e-mail at hi123@mdp.com or by phone at 800/678-2093.

Contacting the Home Depot

For general information about product availability contact your local Home Depot or visit The Home Depot website at www.homedepot.com.

Bathroom Accessories

American Standard
800/422-1902
www.americanstandard.com

Bath Unlimited
800/635-2731
www.bathunlimited.com

Focus Products Group (Jerdon)
972/690-4286

Glacier Bay
Exclusively through
The Home Depot®
www.glacierbayinfo.com

Hinge-It
800/284-4643
www.hingeit.com

Kimball & Young
800/639-6864
www.kimballyoung.com

Kohler Co.
800/456-4537
www.kohler.com

Stanley Furniture
276/627-2540
www.stanleyfurniture.com

Cabinetry & Hardware

Decolav, Inc.
561/274-2110
www.decolav.com

Inhabit
888/830-5072
www.inhabitliving.com

Kohler Co.
800/456-4537
www.kohler.com

KraftMaid Cabinetry
888/562-7744
www.kraftmaid.com

Thomasville Cabinetry
800/756-6497
www.thomasvillecabinetry.com

Tri-City Glass
800/521-5221
www.tricityglass.com

Zenith Interiors
800/892-3986
www.zenith-interiors.com

Countertops

DuPont Corian
www.corian.com

Silestone by Cosentino
800/291-1311
www.silestoneusa.com

Flooring

Daltile
800/933-8453
www.daltileproducts.com

Metroflor
203/299-3100
www.metroflorusa.com

Tarkett
888/639-8275
www.tarkett-floors.com/us/

Lighting

Eurofase Inc.
www.eurofase.com

Hampton Bay
www.homedepot.com

Progress Lighting
864/599-6000
www.progresslighting.com

Plumbing & Fixtures

Delta Faucet Company
800/345-3358
www.deltafaucet.com

Kohler Co.
800/456-4537
www.kohler.com

Moen
800/289-6636
www.moen.com

Price Pfister
800/732-8238
www.pricepfister.com

Sinks, Showers, Toilets, & Tubs

American Standard
800/442-1902
www.americanstandard.com

Decolav, Inc.
561/274-2110
www.decolav.com

Delta Faucet Company
www.deltafaucet.com
800/345-3358

Grohe America, Inc.
630/582-7711
www.groheamerica.com

Kohler Co.
800/456-4537
www.kohler.com

Mirabella Imports LLC
310/783-7660
www.mirabellaimports.com

Pittsburgh Corning
800/624-2120
www.pittsburghcorning.com

Tri-City Glass
www.tricityglass.com

United States Ceramic
800/321-0684
www.usctco.com

resources

Listed on the following pages are the names and manufacturers of the products from the seven bathrooms designed and constructed exclusively from items available from The Home Depot® and that are featured in the first chapter of this book. To determine whether an item shown in the book is still available from The Home Depot contact your local store if the item is listed in the resource section. If it is not listed you will often be able to find an equivalent product within The Home Depot's extensive inventory that is newly improved by the manufacturer.

Colors

Please be aware that paint colors shown in the book may look different on your wall because of the printing process used in this book. If you see a color you like, show it to a Home Depot associate in the paint department, and he or she will custom-tint paint to match it as closely as possible. Buy samples of paint in small quantities and test areas so that you can see the result prior to spending time and money to paint the entire room. Changes in lighting affect colors, which, for instance, can seem remarkably different under artificial light and natural light. Also, consult everyone who will be living with the color. Paint a test area and live with it under different lighting conditions for at least 24 hours to make sure it is right for you.

Pages 8–11

Storage Drawer: Kohler Tellieur 14⅝" tall with two drawers, K-3106

Storage Case: Kohler Tellieur 14" tall with textured glass door insert, K-3108-DG

Mirror: Kohler Tellieur, K-3113

Sink: Kohler Iron Works, K-2822-8S

Sink Faucet: Kohler Purist widespread lavatory faucet, K-14406-3

Console Table and Towel Bars: Kohler Iron Works Tellieur console table, K-3116; Kohler Iron Works towel bars for use with K-3116 console table only (pair), K-3118

Pages 8–11 (continued)

Bath: Kohler Iron Works Tellieur, K-727-2S

Bath Fixtures: Kohler Laminar wall- or ceiling-mount bath filler with .08" orifice, K-922; Kohler Purist two-handle bath- or deck-mount trim with lever handles, K-T14429-4

Toilet: Kohler Revival toilet bowl, K-4355; Kohler Iron Works Tellieur toilet tank, K-4401; Kohler Iron Works Tellieur elongated toilet seat, K-4622; Kohler Iron Works Tellieur flush actuator, K-9444

Bidet: Kohler Revival centerset bidet, K-4832; Kohler Taboret lever handles, K-16070-4

Shower Fixtures: Kohler Purist Rite-Temp valve trim, K-T14423-3; Kohler Forte single-function showerhead, K-10282; Kohler Showerarm and flange, 7½" long, K-7397

Tissue Holder: Kohler Purist, K-14444

Robe Hook: Kohler Purist, K-14443

Soap Dish: Kohler Purist, K-14445

Flooring: 24" SQ Stepping Stone in Brick Face, 594-561

Shower Walls: Tri-City Glass, custom glass

Storage Shelves: Tri-City Glass, custom glass

Pages 12–15

Shower Door: Kohler Purist three 6" steam pivot shower door, K-702224-D4

Sink: Kohler DemiLav wading pool lavatory, K-2833

Sink Fixtures: Kohler Purist single-control tall lavatory faucet, K-14404-4

Lighting: Progress Lighting three-light wall light in chrome, P3242-15; IKEA Orgel wall sconces

Bath: Kohler Portrait 5' whirlpool bath, K-1014-H2

Bath Fixtures: Kohler Purist bath- or deck-mount filler trim, K-T14428-4

Toilet: Kohler Glenbury elongated toilet seat, K-4684; Kohler Portrait Comfort Height toilet, K-3357-47

Flooring: Tarkett Signature Sava Slate Resilient sheet vinyl flooring in Vermont Red, #87079

Countertop, Tub Deck, Beams, and Ladder: Custom-made wood

Cabinetry: Kraftmaid custom-made

Towel Bar, Robe Hook, Toilet Paper Holder, Towel Ring: Glacier Bay Double

Mirror: Bath Unlimited Alexandria arched mirror, 62340SN

Pages 16–17

Sink: Kohler Crucible Vessels countertop lavatory, K-2271-R5

Sink Fixtures: Kohler Falling Water wall-mount lavatory faucet trim with 10¼" spout, K-T197-BN

Toilet: Kohler Leighton comfort-height toilet with concealed trapway and left-hand trip lever, less seat, K-3486-0; Kohler French Curve elongated, closed-front toilet seat and cover, K-4653-0

Shower Fixtures: Price Pfister Ashfield brushed nickel, 808-YPOK

Flooring: MetroFlor Versatal Shale vinyl tile in Antique Stone, #10103

Shower Tile: United States Ceramic 4x4" tile in white/matte, U273-44

Shower Block and Sink Base: Pittsburg Corning 8x8x3" clear glass block

Shower Fixtures and Accessories: Kohler Fairfax glass shelf, K-12158; Kohler Fairfax 18" towel bar, K-12150-BN; Kohler Fairfax small towel bar, K-12155-BN; Kohler Fairfax double robe hook, K-12153-BN; Tri-City Glass custom-cut glass on shower walls

Mirror: Stanley beveled edge 36×48"

Tissue Holder: Kohler Fairfax, K-12157-BN

Lighting: Hampton Bay four-light vanity light in etched marble glass and brushed nickel

Blinds: Springs DSP Graber Grandeur 2" aluminum, GGA2X

Bath Shelves and Linen Tower: Zenith Interiors Studio Accents, 9058SS

Fabric Panel Closet Door: In Habit 24×78" Slat in Grass

Pages 18–21

Sink: Kohler Memoirs undercounter lavatory, K-2339-96

Sink Fixtures: Kohler Finial Art widespread lavatory faucet with wrought swirl handles, K-610-4W

Bath: Kohler Memoirs 5' bath whirlpool with left-hand drain, K-723-H2-96

Bath Fixtures: Kohler Finial Art Rite-Temp pressure-balancing bath and shower faucet trim with wrought swirl handle, K-T612-4W

Toilet: Kohler Memoirs comfort-height toilet seat, K-3453-96; Kohler Glenbury elongated toilet seat, K-4684

Robe Hook: Kohler Finial Art, K-623-TB

Towel Bar: Kohler Finial Art 24", K-618

Tissue Holder: Kohler Finial Art, K-619

Flooring/Walls in Shower and Bath: 3×10" Romance Almond bullnose, 489-198; 10×13" Romance Almond, 902-682; 3×10" Romance Listellos, 489-220; 13×13" Romance Almond, 904-576

Cabinets: Thomasville Plaza door-style open and closed storage in Cider Maple and Cinnamon Cherry with a combination of finishes

Cabinet Hardware: Thomasville pull, M207; knob, M366

Countertops: Silestone mahogany with backsplash, 243-616

Pages 22–23

Lavatory: Kohler Bancroft, K2348-8-Y2

Pedestal: Kohler Bancroft, K2346-Y2

Lavatory Supply: Kohler, K-7605-P-SN

P-Trap: Kohler, K-9018-SN

Bath: Kohler Bancroft whirlpool bath, K-1151-RA-Y2

Drain: Kohler bath drain, K7161-AF-SN

Trim Kit: Kohler, K-9698-SN

Keypad Trim: Kohler, K-9497-SN

Faucet: Kohler Bancroft lavatory faucet, K10577-4-SN

Toilet: Kohler Bancroft toilet bowl, K-4281-Y2; Kohler Bancroft toilet tank, K-4633-Y2; Kohler toilet seat, K-4659-Y2; Kohler toilet supply, K-7637-SN

Trip Lever: Kohler, K-9475-SN

Shower/Bath Trim: Kohler Bancroft shower, K-T10581-4-SN

Valve: Kohler, K-304-K-NA

Bath Door: Kohler Fluence, K-702206-L-MX

Towel Bar: Kohler, K-11416-SN

Robe Hook: Kohler, K11414-SN

Shower and Bath Tile: United States Ceramic Fifth Avenue 3×6" subway tile in white, 072-36

Paint: Behr in honey beige, 390D-4

Floor: Armstrong Vinyl, Saddle Memories

Lights: Hampton Bay sconce in brushed nickel, 469-231

Mirror: Stanley 30×36" frameless polished edge mirror, 922-834

Pages 30–31

Cabinets: MasterBath Raised-Panel in black

Cabinet Hardware: Amerock Manor satin nickel knob, BP26131-G10

Sink: Kohler Memoirs in self-rimming in white, K-2241

Faucet: Kohler Memoirs, brushed chrome, K-454-4V

Medicine Cabinet: MasterBath medicine cabinet 24" swing door in black

Countertop: DuPont Corian in Bone

Towel Bar: Kohler Memoirs 23" brushed chrome, K-486

Lighting: Progress Lighting Glenmont two-light in brushed nickel, P3136-09

Toilet: Kohler Cimarron comfort-height elongated in white, K-3496

Floor and Floor Tile: Brancacci Windrift in beige

Shower Receptor: Kohler Kathryn cast iron in Biscuit, K-9025

Showerheads: Kohler Memoirs multi-function showerhead in brushed chrome, K-444; Kohler shower arm in brushed chrome, K-7397; Kohler handshower, K-419

Bodyspray Tiles: Kohler WaterTile in brushed chrome, K-8002

Shower trim: Kohler Memoirs in brushed chrome, K-9695

Shower door: Sterling Finesse by-pass in chrome, 5375-48S

Tub: Kohler Devonshire whirlpool tub in white, K-1357

Tub Filler: Kohler Memoirs in brushed chrome, K-T469 4VG

Pages 32–35

Toilet: Kohler Kathryn Comfort Height toilet bowl, less seat, K-4258-0; Kohler Kathryn toilet tank, K-4403-0; Kohler Kathryn toilet seat with polished chrome hinges, K-4701-CP-0

Console Table: Kohler Kathryn 42" enameled lavastone console table top with 10" centers, K-3028-K3; Kohler Kathryn square tapered metal legs, K-6861-CP

Sink: Kohler Kathryn undercounter lavatory with glazed underside, K-2297-G-0

Sink Fixtures: Kohler Antique widespread lavatory faucet with six-prong handles, K-108-3-CP

Flooring: Dupont Real Touch Elite laminate in maple, 131-441

Shower and Tub Fixtures: Elizabethan Classics Chrome showerhead, ESSHSUN CP; Elizabethan Classics chrome tub filler and shower system, ECTW18 CP

Tub: Elizabethan Classics Dual Imperial cast iron clawfoot tub in chrome, D1CP

Lighting: Hampton Bay four-light chandelier, 534-415

Wall Mirror: Stanley Decorative, 202-402

Tissue Holder: Glacier Bay Norfolk

Towel Bar: Glacier Bay Norfolk 18"

index

a-b

Accent lighting, 157
Accessibility, 64–67, 125
Accessories, 25, 27, 150–151, 173, 174
Acrylic tubs, 103
Ambient lighting, 156–157
Art Deco style, 24–27, 158
Asian style, 47, 75, 76, 78, 140, 177
Attic conversions, 32–35, 46, 51, 87, 167
Baskets, 137, 144, 145
Bathtubs. *See also* Whirlpool tubs
  claw-foot style, 32, 105, 174
  contemporary style, 75, 78–79
  fiberglass, 103
  as focal point, 8–9
  freestanding styles, 8–9, 32–33,
    81–82, 104, 105, 107
  materials, 103
  old-world style, 80–83
  overflowing style, 102
  on platforms, 62, 101, 103
  selection of, 100, 103
  under sloping ceilings, 46
  for small spaces, 48
  soaking styles, 39, 41, 100, 164
  traditional style, 72
Beaded board, 46, 72, 94
Bidets, 124, 125
Blackboards, inside medicine
  cabinets, 149
Bookcases, 176
Brass faucets, 119, 122
Bronze faucets, 123

c

Cabinets. *See also* Custom
    cabinets; Vanities
  cleaning tips, 147
  fixed vs. freestanding, 146
  for grooming products, 138
  hardware choices, 152–153
  materials and quality, 137, 139
  semicustom, 137, 139
  stock, 137, 139
Candles, 30, 173
Casement windows, 165
Cast-polymer tubs, 103
Ceilings, 13, 32, 46
Center-set faucets, 119
Ceramic tile
  countertops, 91, 92
  floors, 19, 86
  walls, 94
Chandeliers, 32, 83
Chrome faucets, 120, 122
Claw-foot tubs, 32, 105, 174
Closets, 16, 43, 137
Coffee bars, 174, 178
Color schemes
  blue and white, 49
  citrus green, 32–35
  lavender, 41
  and mood, 73
  for small spaces, 51
  spa style, 173
  white, 71
  yellow and white, 23
Concrete sinks, 115
Console sinks, 116
Contemporary style, 12–15, 74–79,
  114–115, 140–141, 143, 152
Countertops
  ceramic tile, 91, 92
  extended, 51
  glass, 92, 93, 114
  granite, 90, 113
  laminate, 91
  lavastone, 35

limestone, 90
  quartz, 21
  slate, 91
  solid-surface, 91, 92
  stainless-steel, 92
  stone, 92
  types of, 91–93
Country style, 55, 145
Custom cabinets
  benefits of, 137
  examples of, 18–21, 72, 132–133,
    145, 146, 147
  mixing finishes, 18–21
  Custom-made showers, 107

d-f

Design checklist, 61–63
Double-hung windows, 165
Drawer pulls, 152–153
Electric outlets, 67
Enameled cast-iron tubs, 103
Enameled steel tubs, 103
European style, 53, 80–83, 182
Exhaust fans, 169
Expansion, of space, 49, 51
Family baths, 44–47
Fans, 168–169
Faucets
  coordination of sink with tub, 123
  dark color, 63
  finish, 120, 122–123
  placement of, 30, 119
  spread-fit, 119, 121, 123
  types of, 24, 118–123
  vintage style, 34, 44, 116, 119
  wallmount style, 100, 113, 119
  for whirlpool tubs, 30
Fiberglass tubs, 103

g-l

m-q

r-s